Born Storytellers

Born Storytellers

Readers Theatre Celebrates the Lives and Literature
of Classic Authors

Ann N. Black

Teacher Ideas Press, an imprint of Libraries Unlimited
Westport, Connecticut • London

Library of Congress Cataloging-in-Publication Data

Black, Ann N.
  Born storytellers : Readers theatre celebrates the lives and literature of
classic authors / Ann N. Black.
    p. cm.
  Includes bibliographical references and index.
  ISBN 1–59469–003–0 (pbk. : alk. paper)
  1. Authors—Drama. 2. Authorship—Drama. 3. Young adult drama, American.
4. Biographical drama. I. Title.
PS3602.L245B67   2005
808.5'3—dc22   2005016059

British Library Cataloguing in Publication Data is available.

Library of Congress Catalog Card Number: 2005016059
ISBN:1–59469–003–0

First published in 2005

Libraries Unlimited/Teacher Ideas Press, 88 Post Road West, Westport, CT 06881
A Member of the Greenwood Publishing Group, Inc.
www.lu.com

Printed in the United States of America

The paper used in this book complies with the
Permanent Paper Standard issued by the National
Information Standards Organization (Z39.48-1984).

10   9   8   7   6   5   4   3   2   1

For Bob—Sonnet LXXVIII and "love remembr'd"

Contents

Acknowledgments

My thanks to Tutt Library of Colorado College; to the staff and readers from Teen Volunteers of Pikes Peak Library District; to my critique partners, Marty Banks, Linda DuVal, Maria Faulconer, Toni Knapp, and Susan Rust, for their invaluable suggestions and enthusiasm; to Cody Rust for his art and Dr. Casey Black for his translation; to Hugh for "a sea of faith" trans-Atlantic; and to my sons, Robert, William, and Casey for their eagle eyes and confidence. And for her editorial wisdom and friendly patience, my deep appreciation to Suzanne Barchers.

Introduction

Welcome to *Born Storytellers*, a set of readers theatre scripts with a unique oral approach to classic literature for young people. A distinct pattern shapes the intent and form of these scripts—they investigate, connect, and dramatize.

Using kid-friendly dialogue, these ten scripts probe the lives and backgrounds of classic authors, seeking the sources of their imagination and talent. These discoveries are then linked to excerpts of their classical writing. With this rich understanding of both the writer and the work, the literature springs to life for the readers and the audience.

Oral interpretation of literature is an art, enjoyable, enlightening, and inspiring. As Wallace A. Bacon writes, "Interpretation is an excellent way to studying literature because it *demands* that the student perceive. . . . Passivity is a completely impossible state for the oral reader."[1]

"Why Do We Have to Read *That*?"

This question is all too common. "Unseasoned, shaky readers sit in every school, unable to enjoy or even comprehend the literature assignments before them."[2] Many don't read at all. So it is not surprising to learn that a 2004 survey for the National Endowment for the Arts (NEA) found a decline in reading throughout the country.

"*Reading at Risk: A Survey of Literary Reading in America* reports drops in all groups studied, with the steepest rate of decline—28 percent—occurring in the youngest age groups." Dana Gioia, Chairman of the NEA said, "No single factor caused this problem. No single solution can solve it. But it cannot be ignored and must be addressed."[3]

Today, literature is typically approached silently, both within the schoolroom and outside it. The teacher may read passages aloud, but the students by and large read their assignments silently, privately. How can we make literature mean something to these students—encourage them to read?

Suppose we choose a handful of students for a readers theatre group. With scripts from *Born Storytellers* in hand and with performance in mind, these students will discover for themselves the despair of Edgar Allan Poe, the fantasies of Shakespeare, or the dreams of Jules Verne. Then, with the author's own story fully in mind, the written words of the literature will become the oral words of the readers.

When our readers are ready to perform, they will be sharing information and bringing art to life. Their fellow students in the audience—who might otherwise be dozing and drifting along, uninterested—now listen, watch, and respond. Silence is no longer golden. A literary activity, formerly dull and dormant, has become vibrant and interactive.

Readers theatre presentations, with their emphasis on oral reading, offer dramatic solutions to the presentation of literature. Indeed, *Born Storytellers* presents a jump-start into the classic authors and their literature, stimulating students' imaginations and heightening their interests in reading more and writing better.

Readers Theatre: What It Is; What It Is Not

Readers theatre implies that two or more oral readers present literature to an audience in a staged situation. The readers, using their voices and their bodies, convey the author's intent inherent in the words.

Readers theatre in the school setting blossoms with this artful simplicity. Performances can be held anywhere—in the classroom, in the community room, or on a stage. Such adaptability eliminates jockeying for rehearsal or performance space, and free of elaborate production requirements, readers theatre can be an appropriate program for class projects and special events and even a unique entry for contest work.

Readers theatre scripts are not only easy to produce, they are also student-inclusive. Casting does not depend on appearance. This is especially heartwarming for students who are not yet mature. Sense and feelings matter, not height or weight. The eyes have it—and the voices.

The unique performance aspects of readers theatre can build confidence. Students who are reluctant to perform will respond in a more positive manner when they understand the ease and simplicity of performing with a script—one that does not have to be memorized, yet must be read well.

Striving for fluent, intelligible reading, students pay attention to punctuation when they read aloud. They begin to sense the power of verbs that heighten their reading and animate the author's meaning. They enlarge their vocabularies. They learn to articulate unfamiliar words that may come from another time or place.

Reading orally, students sharpen their communications skills. They learn to project their voices and the emotions behind the writing. They discover the values in pacing, inflection and the build up and release of tension. They practice quick response to other readers. Now, even the shyest, most reluctant reader is part of a group effort in sharing literature with an expectant audience.

As they perfect their work, the students realize the control they have. They are creating another world with another person's language. For a few moments they can become Daniel Defoe describing a shipwreck, Louisa May Alcott mourning the death of Beth, Rudyard Kipling racing through the Kashmir bazaar or Charles Dickens shuddering in the graveyard.

Although provocative and entertaining, readers theatre does not embrace the more comprehensive art form of conventional theatre, where dramatic literature vivified by actors is usually heightened by decorative, visual, and auditory effects. Readers theatre does not rely on costumes, lighting, scenery, props, or sound and music effects.

However, the benefits of readers theatre do extend to other arts that express ideas and emotions through words. For example, the process of creative writing takes on new meaning when classic authors are read aloud. Surprising questions about form and style and language arise: How did the author describe that view, twist that plot, hear that old man speak? How does that story begin? Why does it end that way? What touched me in the story? Where did those characters come from?

"To understand the thoughts of another mind, fixed in print, to read beyond one's own experience, means to identify with that mind, to learn the physical satisfactions or frustrations behind it, and to understand the ideas and emotions that have evolved from it."[4] It is no accident that Leslie Irene Coger and Melvin R. White have identified readers theatre as "Theatre of the Mind."[5] Readers theatre, then, inspires creative reading and writing for readers and audience members alike.

But What About the Audience?

Every audience has expectations—mainly to be entertained. But when witnessing the successful oral interpretation of a literary script, an audience will find itself imagining—responding both emotionally and intellectually to the performance and, above all, to the literature.

Students need clues before witnessing a performance. They need encouragement to listen closely, to visualize who and what they are going to hear. They need information: What is readers theatre? What is the subject? What is the protocol? When do we clap? Once suggestions are given and expectations shaped, the student audience can respond easily to the readers and the literature they are about to hear.

Where Do You Start?

You start with enthusiasm, of course, because readers theatre is a gratifying project for the teacher and fun for the students when certain procedures and concerns are addressed.

First, choose and prepare the script. All the scripts in this book are of the same length, planned to accommodate a typical class period. Two pages of introductory material for the teacher, plus any special instructions, precede each script.

The exact number of scripts and black folders needed are listed on each "Presentation" page. However, to compensate for lost or forgotten pages, or for those "the dog ate it" excuses, it is wise to make an extra copy. When copying the scripts, it might be expedient to use three-hole-punched paper for the black folders.

Cast members can keep track of their parts easily if they highlight their lines—for example, blue for Storyteller 1, yellow for Storyteller 2, and so on.

Second, choose the cast. Casts range in number from seven to twenty-two. Most parts can be read by boys or by girls. Lines are fairly evenly divided among the characters. Generally, it is a good idea to make temporary assignments of the individual parts at first. Then another one or two read-throughs should indicate ideal choices for the permanent assignments.

Third, locate the stage props. Presentation instructions suggest reading stands, which are very helpful. When reading stands are available, loose script pages are less of a problem. Sometimes music stands can be borrowed for the readers. Tall stools or chairs make it easy for the audience to see the readers.

Rehearsal Time

Cast members will need a quick briefing on readers theatre before work begins. By this time, of course, the teacher has introduced the literary subject and author of the chosen script. Then an explanation of what we are going to do and how we are going to do it is in order.

The cast of a *Born Storytellers* presentation will be performing the classics—as themselves—in a new and entertaining way. Most students will be happy they do not have to be concerned about costumes and makeup. Best of all, they do not have to memorize their parts. But they do have an obligation. Readers theatre requires complete familiarity with the script. Readers must read well for their audience.

A brief definition of the expected audience might follow, as should any particular logistical details. For example, the teacher presents the time frame for rehearsals and performances and outlines the schedule for individual study and group work.

During rehearsals, in addition to mastering the lines of the script, students will want to practice a few physical actions that are appropriate for readers theatre. Rehearsing with the stools or chairs in performance position will help establish the desired moods of the script.

Further, in order to stress certain lines, scenes, or situations, the teacher may want to incorporate directions for sitting and standing during the performance. Generally speaking, readers do not move about the stage. They may use their hands, but their facial expressions and the use of their eyes will highlight their reading.

Where do the readers look when they are performing? Establishing that focus begins in rehearsal. Rule of thumb: They look out and over the heads of the audience. At times, focus can shift from the center of the audience to the right side, the left side, or back again—but always over the heads of the listeners. At times, onstage focus may be appropriate. More pronounced shifts depend on individual lines. For example, one reader may address another momentarily for special emphasis.

Establishing the tone of the performance begins during the first readings of the script. At the outset and throughout the scripts, dialogue of an informal nature provides a smooth continuity between the expository material and the literary excerpts. Readers, using their best interpretative techniques and qualities, will demonstrate their understanding of the background material and apply their sensitivity to the author's intent as they become the voice for his or her classic writing.

Performance Time

An imaginary curtain goes up. The stage or performance space is set with reading stands and stools or chairs. Readers, perhaps dressed in similar or uniform colors, are ready to make their entrance. Accessories and clothing that may detract from the reading have been discouraged. The cue is given, and the readers enter, carrying their scripts onstage in a prearranged fashion. They take their positions, and if they have a reading stand, they place their scripts on it. They look down until the Announcer enters. On a prearranged cue during the Announcer's first lines, the readers look up. The performance has begun.

Finally, to cap the dramatic presentation, the performance should end with a flair. The Announcer's last speech will clue in the audience. Then, the applause begins. The readers close their scripts. They bow their heads for a moment. Again, on a prearranged cue, the readers exit the performance space in the same manner as they entered—but smiling now after their resounding success.

Notes

General note: Quotation marks in the literary excerpts have been eliminated and slight punctuation changes have been made to facilitate the flow of oral reading.

1. Bacon, Wallace A., *The Art of Interpretation* (New York: Holt, Rinehart and Winston, 1966), 6.

2. Black, Ann N., "A Literary Commune" (master's thesis, University of North Texas, 1974), 36.

3. National Endowment of the Arts, July 8, 2004. http://arts.endow.gov/news/news04/ReadingAtRisk.html. Accessed July 24, 2004.

4. Black, "A Literary Commune," 32.

5. Coger, Leslie Irene, and White, Melvin R., *Readers Theatre Handbook: A Dramatic Approach to Literature* (Glenview, IL: Scott, Foresman, 1967), 10.

Louisa May Alcott and *Little Women*— Double Image

Invincible Louisa May! Born into poverty and brilliance, the dynamic Louisa May Alcott created a classic world for young girls from the real pages of her life.

The latter part of the nineteenth century proved a fertile ground for both English and American novelists. We think of Charles Dickens, Jules Verne, Daniel Defoe. We remember Mark Twain, Harriet Beecher Stowe, Kate Chopin, and—Louisa May Alcott. Ambition, talent, or money urged on many of these authors, but the background and nucleus of their training and education certainly helped to shape their skills.

Louisa May Alcott lived among some of the greatest minds of the 1800s. The writer, teacher, and philosopher Amos Bronson Alcott was her father. Friends and members of his academic circle, such as Ralph Waldo Emerson and Henry David Thoreau, participated in her education. The intellectual air she breathed in Concord and Boston contributed immeasurably to her broad thinking. In addition, the staunch faith that characterized her family influenced her personal life and directed her writing.

She served as a nurse in the Union Army. She was the first woman to vote in Concord. Following her mother's precepts, she instigated philanthropic ventures for diverse causes, such as improved orphanages for boys and better prisons for women.

Determined to succeed with her writing, she poured out story after story for five or ten dollars—until she caught the brass ring with her heartwarming novel, *Little Women*. Never marrying, she became a generous aunt, even raising her niece after her sister May died.

Born on her father's birthday, Louisa May Alcott died March 6, 1888, at age fifty-five, two days after her father's funeral.

Presentation of Louisa May Alcott Script

Sentiment and gentle humor go hand in hand within Louisa May Alcott's classic novel, *Little Women*. Young people may come to this book for the first time via the movies. Others, from the dusty shelves kept by mothers who still remember and treasure the gaiety and tragedy of the March family who faced all odds with indomitable spirit.

Louisa May Alcott lived this novel before it was ever born, for its characters and plot stem from her own family life. The enduring success of *Little Women* surely demonstrates to all writers, young and old, that famous adage, "Write what you know."

The format of this script shows the intertwining of Alcott's real life with her novel. For this reason, when the performance begins, all Storytellers are seated, but they stand when they quote from *Little Women*. For example, Storytellers 3 and 4, who only handle exposition and comments, do not stand until they are excited at the very end.

The script calls for an all-girl cast of nine readers, including the Announcer. However, boys could be cast as Storytellers 1 and 2 or as the Announcer.

Stage Props

8 reading stands, if possible

8 tall stools or chairs

Hand Props

9 scripts (plus 1 for the teacher)

9 black folders for scripts

Louisa May Alcott and *Little Women*—Double Image

```
        X       X       X
        1    Louisa May  2

  X       X       X                  X    X
 Anna  Elizabeth   May                3    4

                 Announcer
```

Announcer: *(Announcer takes center stage)* Welcome to Storyteller Theatre—where we find the classic books and their classic authors who rise to greet us. Today we will meet a most unusual woman who wrote stories about the people she knew best—her own family and herself. We're speaking, of course, about the double image of Louisa May Alcott and her powerful book, *Little Women*.

Storyteller 3: Oh, no! *Little Women*? I know I'm going to cry!

Announcer: Why would you do that? I thought you loved *Little Women*.

Storyteller 3: *(Sniffling already)* Oh, I do! I love it.

Storyteller 4: I understand that. My mother says she always cries at weddings.

Louisa May: *(Smiles at Storyteller 3)* Happiness and sadness—the warp and woof of family life.

Announcer: *(To Storyteller 3)* You see? Louisa May Alcott understood those emotions. *(To Louisa May)* Didn't you, Miss Alcott?

Louisa May: I think I did. Certainly my family enjoyed both.

Storyteller 4: You enjoyed being sad?

Louisa May: *(Laughs)* I'm afraid the Alcotts were the original Pathetic Family.

Storyteller 4: Oh, that is sad, Miss Alcott. You must have suffered a great deal—to call your family pathetic.

Louisa May: Well, it's true we did struggle. Life was hard. We were poor. For years we ate meals of plain boiled rice without sugar or hot graham meal without butter or molasses. None of us tasted meat until we were grown.

Announcer: That is pathetic.

Louisa May: Perhaps, but that's not what I mean by pathetic. I mean my family embraced every part of life. We felt deeply every sad event. Yet we could feel so happy when life was rich and good.

Announcer: The Greeks have a word for that, *pathetikos*—capable of feeling.

Storyteller 4: You have to say the March family in *Little Women* feels a lot.

Storyteller 3: *(Still sniffling)* Oh, the March family is very *pathetikos*!

Announcer: All right. I think we're prepared now to laugh or cry. So, let's flip back the calendar to the eighteen-hundreds—to Miss Alcott, to her family, and to their double image in *Little Women*. Listen! *(Exits)*

Anna: My name is Anna Alcott. I was a toddler when my sister Louisa was born. We were living in Germantown, Pennsylvania. I believe that's part of Philadelphia now, isn't it, Weedy?

Louisa May: *(Smiles at Anna)* Philadelphia, yes, and that ridiculous nickname you dreamed up for me—Weedy. Louisa—*Weedy? (Shrugs)* Well, what's in a name? Anna and I were practically babies together and quite inseparable. She was only two when I was born—on Father's birthday, November 29, 1832.

Anna: Then three years later, we had a baby sister.

Elizabeth: That was me—Elizabeth. *(Smiles)* Louisa May's the writer and my beloved sister. She, too, was a toddler when I was born—1835—making us a family of five. Marmee, our wonderful mother, kept us together while Father ran a school for young people. He worked very hard, and he was very bright—but the school was not very successful.

May: So Father had to close the school and move our family all the way to Concord, Massachusetts, where I was born—in 1840. *(Smiles)* I was the fourth girl for Father and Marmee. They named me Abigail May, after Marmee, but they called me May.

Storyteller 4: The Alcotts—the original Pathetic Family—Anna, Louisa May, Elizabeth, May and their parents. So let's visit the March family in *Little Women* and meet those girls.

Anna: *(Stands)* In the book, Louisa calls me Meg.

Storyteller 1: *(Stands)* Margaret, the eldest of the four, was sixteen, and very pretty, being plump and fair, with large eyes . . . soft, brown hair, a sweet mouth, and white hands, of which she was rather vain.

Louisa May: And I become Jo—not exactly my alter ego—more like another print of the same picture. *(Stands)* Fifteen-year-old Jo was very tall, thin, and brown, and reminded one of a colt, for she never seemed to know what to do with her long limbs. . . . She had a decided mouth, a comical nose, and sharp, gray eyes. . . . Her long, thick hair was her one beauty, but it was usually bundled into a net, to be out of the way. *(Sits)*

Storyteller 3: Jo becomes romantic in the book. *(Pause)* Like you, Miss Alcott?

Louisa May: *(Laughs)* Perhaps. Perhaps Jo is my own self—though it is true I never married. Nor did I want to. Too many responsibilities.

Elizabeth: Or too much ambition? Louisa burned with that. She wanted to write stories and sell them—to make money for us. I admired her so much—loved her so much. I am Elizabeth in her book. *(Stands)*

Storyteller 1: Beth, as everyone called her, was a rosy, smooth-haired, bright-eyed girl of thirteen with a shy manner, a timid voice, and a peaceful expression, which was seldom disturbed.

May: My turn! Louisa sort of changed my name. She turned M-a-y into A-m-y and called me Amy in her book. Then she drew a rather artistic portrait of me. *(Stands)*

Storyteller 2:	*(Stands)* Amy, though the youngest, was a most important person—in her own opinion at least. A regular snow maiden, with blue eyes and yellow hair curling on her shoulders, pale and slender, and always carrying herself like a young lady mindful of her manners.
Louisa May:	*(Stands)* Amy was the truest artist of us all. But no matter what talents or private hopes we might have, we four girls were bound to follow Marmee's guidelines:
Anna:	Rule yourself.
Elizabeth:	Love your neighbor.
May:	Do the duty which lies nearest you.
Louisa May:	*(Sits)* Our mothers's version, I think, of *The Pilgrim's Progress.*
Storyteller 3:	Should I know that book?
Louisa May:	It's a wonderful story—an allegory—Christian fighting his way to heaven. We girls loved acting it out. *(Smiles)* But then, we loved acting—drama. I actually wanted to become an actress—to go on the stage—but it was not an idea that went down very well.
Storyteller 4:	But you girls never complained of being poor? Never?
Louisa May:	Well, sometimes. *(Smiles)* And I could be the worst of all. I remember one Christmas in particular. It aroused such strong feelings in me that I had to put that Christmas in my book.
Storyteller 3:	Oh, I remember that scene in *Little Women*. Play it for us, please.
Louisa May:	We will. In fact, I will begin and you can help. *(Stands, then begins to read)* "Christmas won't be Christmas without any presents," grumbled Jo, lying on the rug.
Anna:	"It's so dreadful to be poor!" sighed Meg.
May:	I don't think it's fair for some girls to have plenty of pretty things, and other girls nothing at all.
Elizabeth:	We've got Father and Mother and each other.
Storyteller 1:	The four young faces on which the firelight shone brightened at the cheerful words, but darkened again as Jo said sadly—
Louisa May:	We haven't got Father, and shall not have him for a long time.
Storyteller 1:	She didn't say *perhaps never*, but each was thinking it, thinking of Father far away, where the fighting was.
Storyteller 3:	*(To Storyteller 4)* Fighting? We must be into the Civil War.
Storyteller 4:	We are. It is 1861. The war has just begun. And the father in *Little Women*, Mr. March, is a chaplain in the Union Army.
Anna:	You know the reason Mother proposed not having any presents this Christmas was because it is going to be a hard winter for everyone; and she thinks we ought not to spend money for pleasure, when our men are suffering so in the army.
Louisa May:	But I don't think the little we should spend would do any good. We've each got a dollar, and the army wouldn't be much helped by our giving that. . . . Jo immediately sat up, put her hands in her pockets and began to whistle.

May:	Don't Jo, it's so boyish!
Louisa May:	That's why I do it!
Anna:	You are old enough to . . . behave better, Josephine. It didn't matter so much when you were a little girl; but now you are so tall, and turn up your hair . . . remember that you are a young lady.
Louisa May:	I'm not! And if turning up my hair makes me one, I'll wear it in two tails till I'm twenty.
Storyteller 1:	And Jo pulled off her hair net and shook down a chestnut mane.
Louisa May:	(*Still fretting*) I hate to think I've got to grow up, and be Miss March, and wear long gowns, and look as prim as a China aster! It's bad enough being a girl . . . for I'm dying to go and fight with Papa, and I can only stay at home and knit, like a poky old woman!
Storyteller 1:	And Jo shook the blue army sock till the needles rattled like castanets, and her ball bounded across the room.
Anna:	I think it was so splendid of Father to go as a chaplain when he was too old to be drafted and not strong enough for a soldier.
Louisa May:	Don't I wish I could go as a drummer . . . or a nurse, so I could be near and help him.
Storyteller 4:	Wait. Wait, Miss Alcott. Didn't *you* really become an Army nurse?
Louisa May:	(*Sits*) I did. Like Jo, I was determined to do something positive to help the war effort. So, one day, I took the train to Washington, D.C., and signed up to become a nurse for the Union Army.
Storyteller 3:	Nursing wounded soldiers? That would be dreadfully hard.
Louisa May:	Well, I wanted to serve the Union Cause. Help was needed, and I loved nursing. Unfortunately, I served only six weeks. I contracted typhoid pneumonia and had to return home.
Storyteller 4:	You always had a strong constitution. Did you recover quickly?
Louisa May:	Not this time. The fever and the medications were too much. My nerves were shattered, and I never again knew the fullness of life and health. Yet the experiences of those weeks, what I saw—what I did—stayed in my mind and heart forever.
Storyteller 4:	I can tell that from the sketches you wrote. So real!
Storyteller 3:	Oh, did you keep a diary?
Louisa May:	Luckily, I did. I always kept a journal, and the notes I put down helped me to write that little book, *Hospital Sketches*.
Storyteller 4:	Did you go to work in the hospital your very first day?
Louisa May:	I did. It was December 1862. All went well, and I got to Georgetown very tired. Was kindly welcomed, slept in my narrow bed with two other roommates, and on the morrow began my new life by seeing a poor man die at dawn, and sitting all day with a boy with pneumonia and a man shot through the lungs. . . . He is about thirty, I think, tall and handsome, mortally wounded, and dying royally, without reproach, repining or remorse.

Storyteller 3:	That sounds like it's right out of *Pilgrim's Progress*.
Louisa May:	*(Smiles)* Perhaps it does—but these struggles were real. I had to write them down: At nine the bell rings, gas is turned down, and day nurses go to bed. Night nurses go on duty, and sleep and death have the house to themselves.
Storyteller 3:	That gives me the shivers—like the telegram for Mrs. March from the Army hospital in Washington. Jo reads it to everyone:
Louisa May:	*(Stands)* "Mrs. March: Your husband is very ill. Come at once."
Storyteller 2:	Mrs. March . . . stretched out her arms to her daughters, saying in a tone they never forgot—
Storyteller 1:	*(As Marmee)* I shall go at once, but it may be too late. Oh, children, children, help me to bear it!
Anna:	For several minutes there was nothing but the sound of sobbing in the room, mingled with broken words of comfort, tender assurances of help, and hopeful whispers that died away in tears.
Storyteller 1:	*(Continues as Marmee)* Send a telegram saying I will come at once. The next train goes early in the morning. I'll take that. . . . Leave a note at Aunt March's. Jo, give me that pen and paper.
Louisa May:	Tearing off the blank side of one of her newly copied pages, Jo drew the table before her mother, well knowing that money for the long, sad journey must be borrowed, and feeling as if she could do anything to add a little sum for her father.
Storyteller 1:	*(As Marmee)* Jo, run to the rooms, and tell Mrs. King that I can't come. On the way get these things. . . . I must go prepared for nursing. Hospital stores are not always good.
Storyteller 2:	The short afternoon wore away . . . still Jo did not come. Finally she came walking in with a very queer expression of . . . a mixture of fun and fear, satisfaction and regret in it, which puzzled the family as much as did the roll of bills she laid before her mother.
Louisa May:	*(Toward Storyteller 1)* That's my contribution toward making Father comfortable and bringing him home!
Storyteller 1:	*(As Marmee)* My dear, where did you get it? Twenty-five dollars! Jo, I hope you haven't done anything rash?
Louisa May:	No. . . . I didn't beg, borrow, or steal it. I earned it, and I don't think you'll blame me for I only sold what was my own.
Storyteller 2:	As she spoke, Jo took off her bonnet, and a general outcry arose, for all her abundant hair was cut short.
Anna:	Your hair! Your beautiful hair!
May:	Oh, Jo, how could you? Your one beauty.
Storyteller 1:	*(As Marmee)* My dear girl, there was no need of this.
Elizabeth:	She doesn't look like my Jo any more, but I love her dearly for it!
Louisa May:	It doesn't affect the fate of the nation, so don't wail, Beth. It will be good for my vanity. I was getting too proud of my wig. It will do my brains good to have that mop taken off. . . . I'm satisfied, so please take the money and let's have supper.

Storyteller 1:	*(As Marmee)* I'm afraid you will regret it one of these days.
Louisa May:	No, I won't!
May:	What made you do it?
Louisa May:	I was wild to do something for Father. . . . I hadn't the least idea of selling my hair at first. Then, in a barber's window I saw tails of hair with the prices marked; and one . . . not so thick as mine, was forty dollars. It came over me . . . that I had one thing to make money out of, and without stopping to think, I walked in, asked if they bought hair, and what they would give for mine.
Elizabeth:	I don't see how you dared do it.
Anna:	Didn't you feel dreadfully when the first cut came?
Louisa May:	I never snivel over trifles like that. . . . A crop is so comfortable I don't think I shall ever have a mane again.
Storyteller 2:	That night, the younger girls fell asleep, but not Meg and Jo. Jo lay motionless and her sister fancied that she was asleep, till a stifled sob made her exclaim, as she touched a wet cheek—
Anna:	Jo, dear, what is it? Are you crying about Father?
Louisa May:	No, not now.
Anna:	What then?
Louisa May:	My—my hair! . . . I'm not sorry. . . . I'd do it again tomorrow, if I could. It's only the vain, selfish part of me that goes and cries in this silly way. Don't tell anyone, it's all over now. I thought you were asleep, so I just made a little private moan for my one beauty.
Storyteller 4:	That scene with Jo is so real.
Storyteller 3:	It is—almost as if *you'd* sold *your* hair.
Louisa May:	*(Sits)* I never did sell it but I could have—for money, the lack of which was a constant worry. *(Little laugh)* My sisters and I always held this treasure as a possible resource in case of need. In fact, I wrote in my journal that I will pay my debts, if I have to sell my hair to do it.
Storyteller 4:	You paid all your father's debts, too.
Louisa May:	Poor Father—brilliant, kind, hard-working, and loving, but very early on I took up the money cause.
Storyteller 3:	You probably could have taught school.
Louisa May:	Oh, I did—but I hated it! I wanted to write and be paid for that!
Storyteller 4:	And other jobs besides teaching were hard to come by?
Louisa May:	For women—in the 1850s? Impossible. My sisters and I all sewed for other people, but sewing did not pay well. Years later I still fought for women's jobs the same way I fought for the right to vote. But one time as a girl, I actually went into service.
Storyteller 3:	Service? You worked for other people—in their homes?
Louisa May:	I became the companion for the sister of an older gentleman—an event that turned out to be two months of disappointment and painful experience that I

	never forgot. *(Proudly)* But later I wrote a short story about it. It was published, and I was paid for it.
Storyteller 4:	I'm impressed! But what about Jo? Does she go into service, too?
Louisa May:	Yes, after a fashion. *(Stands)* The two oldest girls begged to be allowed to do something toward their own support, at least.
Anna:	Margaret found a place as a nursery governess and felt rich with her small salary.
Louisa May:	Jo happened to suit Aunt March, who was lame and needed an active person to wait upon her.
Storyteller 4:	Ah—she'll serve as a companion, like you did.
Louisa May:	*(Sits)* But she doesn't have quite so harsh a time. I accompanied my charge to Europe, but being in service did not suit me.
Storyteller 1:	And this did not suit Jo at all, but she accepted the place since nothing better appeared and, to everyone's surprise, got on remarkably well with her irascible relative.
Storyteller 4:	Write about what you know, isn't that right, Miss Alcott? You're writing about your family and your experiences. What about Jo? Is she scribbling away, hoping to sell her stories and sketches?
Louisa May:	Indeed she is. Then one day—it happened!
Storyteller 3:	I remember that scene, too! Meg, Beth, and Amy were in the sitting room. The newspapers came, and Jo bounced in, laid herself on the sofa, and affected to read.
Anna:	*(To Louisa May)* Have you anything interesting there?
Louisa May:	*(Stands)* Nothing but a story; won't amount to much, I guess.
May:	Read it aloud; that will amuse us and keep you out of mischief.
Elizabeth:	What's the name?
Louisa May:	"The Rival Painters."
Anna:	That sounds well; read it.
Storyteller 2:	The girls listened with interest, for the tale was romantic, and somewhat pathetic, as most of the characters died in the end.
May:	I like that about the splendid picture.
Anna:	I prefer the lovering part. Viola and Angelo are two of our favorite names, isn't that queer?
Storyteller 3:	She's almost crying, for she thought the *lovering* part was tragical.
Elizabeth:	Who wrote it?
Storyteller 2:	The reader suddenly sat up, cast away the paper, displaying a flushed countenance, and with a funny mixture of solemnity and excitement replied in a loud voice—
Louisa May:	Your sister.
Anna:	You?

May:	It's very good.
Elizabeth:	I knew it! I knew it! Oh, my Jo, I *am* so proud!
Louisa May:	I shall write more, and I *am* so happy *(Pause)*, for in time I may be able to support myself and help the girls. *(Sits)*
Storyteller 4:	That title—"The Rival Painters"—sounds familiar.
Louisa May:	Very observant! That was the first story of mine to be published—and that when I was twenty years old. But, of course, it did not pay me a great deal. Money was still very tight.
Storyteller 3:	Perhaps you could have become a real nurse.
Louisa May:	I did consider that—even before I signed up as an Army nurse—for I had become close to sickness and death in the long, long days when our Beth fought to live.
Storyteller 4:	And those long days of sickness take place in *Little Women*, too?
Storyteller 3:	Oh, they do—long, long days. I always cry in this part. Poor Beth. All she could do was read a little and ply her needle—sew a little, embroider a little.
Storyteller 1:	The March girls didn't realize it at the time, but this peaceful time was given them as preparation for the sad hours to come; for by-and-by, Beth said the needle was "so heavy" and put it down forever.
Louisa May:	*(Stands)* Jo never left her for an hour since Beth had said—
Elizabeth:	I feel stronger when you are here.
Louisa May:	Jo slept on a couch in the room, waking often to renew the fire, to feed, lift, or wait upon the patient creature who seldom asked for anything, and "tried not to be a trouble." All day she haunted the room, jealous of any other nurse, and prouder of being chosen than of any honor her life ever brought her.
Anna:	As Beth had hoped, the "tide went out easily," and in the dark hour before the dawn, on the bosom where she had drawn her first breath, she quietly drew her last, with no farewell but one loving look, one little sigh.
Storyteller 4:	Are these lines right from the book?
Louisa May:	*(Nods and sits)* They are—and from my journal: March 14th. My dear Beth died at three this morning, after two years of patient pain. Last week she put her work away, saying the needle was "too heavy," and having given us her few possessions, made ready for the parting in her own simple, quiet way. For two days she suffered much, begging for ether, though its effect was gone. Tuesday she lay in Father's arms, and called us round her, smiling contentedly.
Elizabeth:	*(Turns to Louisa May, then Anna, then May)* *(Slowly)* All here!
Louisa May:	I think she bid us good-by then, as she held our hands and kissed us tenderly. Saturday she slept, and at midnight became unconscious, quietly breathing her life away till three; then, with one last look of the beautiful eyes, she was gone.
Storyteller 3:	Oh, no. It really happened!
Louisa May:	Oh, yes, it did. It really happened.
Storyteller 4:	It's very sad. *(Pause)* We need something cheery.

Storyteller 3:	Could we talk about the boys—the men? That might be cheery.
Louisa May:	The boys I prefer. I always wanted to open a school for boys. But they do grow up, don't they? The majority of them?
Storyteller 4:	And they marry. Right? What does your diary say about that—about your sisters marrying?
Louisa May:	Ah, yes. The thought of my sisters leaving us for a young man had never occurred to me. Then, on the 7th of April Anna came walking in to tell us she was engaged to John Pratt; so another sister is gone. . . . I moaned in private over my great loss; and said I'd never forgive John for taking Anna from me; but I shall if he makes her happy.
Storyteller 3:	In *Little Women*, Meg, just like Anna, brags about her fiancé:
Anna:	Now, my John was just about perfect, you have to admit. I told Aunt March plainly: "John is good and wise, he's got heaps of talent, he's willing to work and sure to get on, he's so energetic and brave. Everyone likes and respects him, and I am proud to think he cares for me, though I'm so poor and young and silly."
Storyteller 4:	But John Pratt did make Anna happy, and you did get over it.
Louisa May:	I did. *(Smiles)* And Jo gets over the loss of Meg with the help of the boy next door—Laurie, who tries to console Jo:
Storyteller 2:	*(As Laurie)* You don't look festive, ma'am, what's the matter?
Louisa May:	*(Stands)* I don't approve of the match, but I've made up my mind to bear it, and shall not say a word against it. . . . *(Pause)* You can't know how hard it is for me to give up Meg.
Storyteller 2:	*(As Laurie)* You don't give her up. You only go halves. . . . You've got me, anyhow. I'm not good for much, I know, but I'll stand by you, Jo, all the days of my life. Upon my word I will! *(Sits)*
Storyteller 4:	Well! *(Smiles at Louisa May)* Now, we need to know all. This Laurie didn't appear to Jo out of nowhere. He must have appeared to our Storyteller first.
Louisa May:	Very perceptive. *(Sits)* I have written many mystery stories, thrillers, scary, sensational things, pot boilers. But I must say my best work has come from what I did, who I knew, what I know.
Storyteller 4:	So—who was the original Laurie that you knew?
Louisa May:	It was a long time ago. *(Pause)* But you're right. Jo's Laurie in *Little Women* was inspired by another Laurie—a Polish lad, a wonderful pianist I met in Switzerland.
Storyteller 3:	This is romantic already. I can feel it! What was his name?
Louisa May:	Ladislas Wisinewski, but we called him Laddie—or Laurie.
Storyteller 3:	There, I knew it! But after Switzerland, then what did you do?
Louisa May:	He met me in Paris where I spent the days in seeing sights with my Laddie, the evenings in reading, writing, hearing "my boy" play, or resting.
Storyteller 3:	And then? *(Pause, more insistent)* And then?
Louisa May:	He came to America, and we talked—and I remembered. His words to me then became Laurie's words to Jo later: *(Stands)*

Storyteller 2:   *(As Laurie)* You *must* hear me. It's no use, Jo, we've got to have it out and the sooner the better for both of us.

Louisa May: Oh . . . I'm so sorry, so desperately sorry. . . . I can't help it. *(Pause)* Laurie, I want to tell you something.

Storyteller 4:   *(Pause)* What? *(Stands)* And then what? What does she tell him?

Storyteller 3:   Oh, oh—I know! *(Stands)* This is where Jo becomes romantic! This is where the *devilish Professor* comes in! Go on!

Announcer: *(Enters to center stage)* Oh, no! Silence! My lips are sealed! Well, until that Professor comes to call. All romance to be continued.

Storyteller 3:   Oh, I think I'm going to cry!

Announcer: Well, check it out again! *Little Women*, by Louisa May Alcott, a born storyteller. *(Bows)* Write what you know, Pilgrims! *(Exits)*

The Surprising Adventures of Daniel Defoe and *Robinson Crusoe*

When Daniel Defoe's novel, *Robinson Crusoe*, was published in 1719, the avid readers who pored through the wonderful adventures frequently mistook the novel as being the autobiography of the author. As tempting as it is to imagine, the truth is even more amazing. It was Daniel Defoe's imagination that created the character of Robinson Crusoe, a man adrift on an island, all alone but determined to survive.

Daniel Defoe's birth date is uncertain—probably 1660, a time of political and religious unrest in England commingled with disasters of disease and fire. Defoe lived through it all, observing, remembering, rebelling, writing. Not until he was in his fifties (old age for the eighteenth century) did he break away from his essays on politics, religion, travel, trade, education, jobs—more than five hundred publications.

Defoe was an inveterate traveler, sometimes for one of his business ventures, sometimes as an informer for political reasons. Married to Mary Tuffley in 1684, Defoe, though famous, struggled financially for most of his life. Then, almost sixty years old, he wrote *Robinson Crusoe*, hailed by many as the first true English novel ever written.

The public was immediately smitten with this tale of a pioneering man, living in isolation and possessing just enough knowledge and just enough supplies to support his determination to stay alive. He was Everyman, and his story was a tremendous success.

Daniel Defoe suffered a stroke (apoplectic attack for those days) and died in 1731. *Robinson Crusoe* is not the story of Defoe, but a basic parallel emerges. Defoe was self-reliant and a man of experience. He brought everything in his life to his imagination. A born storyteller, he created the memorable *Robinson Crusoe*.

Presentation of Daniel Defoe Script

This readers theatre script takes advantage of the truths of Daniel Defoe's life and adventures and interweaves them with the imaginary life and adventures of his character, Robinson Crusoe.

Seven readers, plus the Announcer, make up the cast. Storytellers 1 and 2 flank the reader representing Robinson Crusoe. On the opposite side, Storytellers 3 and 4 support the reader who appears as Daniel Defoe. Positioned between and slightly removed from these two groups is Storyteller 5, who comments and questions various aspects of the script.

Parts for the Storytellers and the Announcer may be read by either boys or girls. Probably best to have boys read for Crusoe and Defoe.

Stage Props

7 reading stands, if possible

7 tall stools or chairs

Hand Props

8 scripts (plus 1 for the teacher)

8 black folders for scripts

1 copy of the book *Robinson Crusoe* for the Announcer to show at the end

The Surprising Adventures of Daniel Defoe and *Robinson Crusoe*

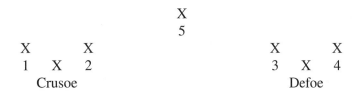

Announcer:	*(Steps to center stage)* Welcome to Storyteller Theatre. Today we tell the tale of two remarkable survivors: Robinson Crusoe and the man who was born to invent his story—Daniel Defoe.
Storyteller 1:	Now there's a survivor—shipwrecked on a desert island!
Storyteller 3:	Who are you talking about?
Storyteller 1:	Who else but Robinson Crusoe? *(Indicates Crusoe, who bows)*
Announcer:	A survivor, indeed—sole survivor, so the story goes. Crusoe survived twenty-eight years on a desert island, off the coast of South America. He could see the mainland, but he had no boat to reach it.
Storyteller 5:	Whoa. He lives alone on a desert island for twenty-eight years?
Announcer:	Well, alone until the last four years—when the cannibals come. Aha. Ready? Two surprising adventure stories, then—Robinson Crusoe's and *(Indicates Defoe)* Daniel Defoe's, our author who created *Robinson Crusoe. (Defoe bows)* Okay? Let's begin! *(Exits)*
Storyteller 5:	Excuse me. Did I hear the word *cannibals* mentioned? Cannibals? The kind that eat people?
Storyteller 2:	That's what they do, all right—especially when they're celebrating.
Storyteller 1:	They celebrate by having a feast.
Storyteller 5:	*(Sings)* "Happy Birthday to you. You're a tough one to chew!"
Storyteller 3:	That's enough! Not funny! Crusoe survives cannibals and more.
Storyteller 4:	We'd like to remind you that Daniel Defoe was a survivor, too.
Storyteller 2:	Mr. Defoe may have been a survivor, but—no offense—he lived in London, a city teeming with people.
Storyteller 4:	Dying people. Haven't you heard of the Great Fire that swept through London—only one year after the Great Plague?
Storyteller 1:	Oh, yes, a terrible disaster that—the Black Death they called it. It raged throughout Europe, then swept across England.
Storyteller 5:	Oh, yuck. An epidemic—worse than the flu! When was this?
Storyteller 4:	More than three hundred years ago—1665, to be exact.

Storyteller 3:	Mr. Defoe was only a child then. About five years old, sir?
Daniel Defoe:	But how I remembered the Plague—the dead bodies, the smell!
Storyteller 4:	Fifty years later, the Plague broke out again, terrifying everyone, and Mr. Defoe wrote about it. He pretended to have been a young man writing during those dreadful times. Sir?
Daniel Defoe:	A dreadful Plague in London was, In the Year Sixty Five, Which swept an Hundred Thousand Souls Away; yet I alive!
Storyteller 3:	He created a diary from his memory, death records and news accounts. He called it *A Journal of the Plague Year*. Listen:
Daniel Defoe:	Innumerable dismal Stories we heard every Day on this Account: Sometimes a Man or Woman dropped down Dead in the very Markets; for many People that had the Plague upon them, knew nothing of it; till the inward Gangreen had affected their Vitals and they dy'd in a few Moments. . . . many died frequently in that Manner in the Streets suddainly, without any warning: Others perhaps had Time to go to . . . any Door, Porch, and just sit down and die.
Storyteller 2:	A realistic journal written fifty years after the Plague? Well, the hero of our book, Robinson Crusoe, tries to keep a journal, too.
Storyteller 1:	Unfortunately, he has very little ink saved from the shipwreck.
Storyteller 5:	Oh, the shipwreck. Tell! That is so exciting!
Storyteller 1:	Okay, think of the map. Think of Africa and South America—the two continents that lie across the South Atlantic Ocean from each other. In the beginning of the book, our man, Robinson Crusoe, is in South America.
Daniel Defoe:	To be exact, he's living and working in Brazil. Crusoe, after several adventures, buys land for a sugar cane plantation—in Brazil. He's become a planter.
Storyteller 1:	First he grows tobacco. He's successful, but he needs workers to help him. So he decides to cross the Atlantic to Africa, buy some servants there, and do some trading.
Storyteller 3:	Ah, to trade! Buy and sell. Import, export. Our man, Defoe, knew something about trade. Tell them, sir:
Daniel Defoe:	Glad to oblige. I started my career working in trade. Trade promoted my success. I encouraged all my readers to reckon well with Trade: Trade is the Wealth of the World. . . . Trade nourishes Industry, Industry begets Trade. True, I started out trading in haberdashery, but I moved on. I moved on!
Storyteller 5:	Haberdashery. I've got that one—he traded in men's socks, gloves, nightcaps, and stuff.
Storyteller 3:	Oh, more than that. Mr. Defoe traded in everything from socks and *stuff* to beer and wine, tobacco, and more.
Storyteller 4:	And he visited the countries he traded with—Holland, Germany, Portugal, Spain. Learned their languages, too.
Daniel Defoe:	I must confess I loved to travel. Had itchy feet all my life.

Storyteller 5:	How did the English travel to these countries—by ship?
Storyteller 2:	Of course. This is the seventeenth century, you know.
Storyteller 5:	I know that! But was Mr. Defoe in a shipwreck like the one he wrote about?
Storyteller 3:	No, but storms destroyed many of his trading ships.
Storyteller 1:	But he was not *personally* in a shipwreck like Robinson Crusoe.
Storyteller 4:	That's true—but reading his book, you can see that he could write about shipwrecks. He could put fear into your heart. Now, begin to imagine: Robinson Crusoe's ship is sailing toward Africa. A hurricane strikes. Men wash overboard. A second storm blows the ship aground. The sea threatens to break the ship in two. The men lower a rowboat and cast off. Listen to this from Robinson Crusoe's diary:
Robinson Crusoe:	We were in a dreadful condition, indeed, and had nothing to do, but to think of saving our lives as well as we could. The wind kept driving us toward the shore. After we had rowed, or rather driven about a league and a half—
Storyteller 5:	A league and a half. Is that about five miles?
Storyteller 3:	I would say that's a good guess.
Robinson Crusoe:	Well, a raging wave, mountain-like, came rolling astern of us, and plainly bade us expect the *coup de grace*.
Storyteller 5:	Got this one, too. *Coo day graw*—the death blow!
Robinson Crusoe:	The wave took us with such fury, that it overset the boat at once; and separating us, as well from the boat as from one another, gave us not time hardly to say, 'O God!' for we were all swallowed up in a moment.
Storyteller 5:	Okay. I'd say that's fear, all right!
Robinson Crusoe:	The wave that came upon me again buried me at once twenty or thirty feet deep . . . and I could feel myself carried with a mighty force and swiftness towards the shore. . . . I was ready to burst with holding my breath, when . . . I found my head and hands shoot out above the surface of the water.
Daniel Defoe:	Then the ocean swamps him again!
Robinson Crusoe:	But I held it out; and finding the water had spent itself, and began to return, I struck forward against the return of the waves, and felt ground . . . with my feet.
Defoe:	He's safe on shore and thanks God he's been saved, but now he ponders his comrades. They were in the rowboat with him.
Robinson Crusoe:	I never saw them afterwards, or any sign of them, except three of their hats, one cap, and two shoes that were not fellows.
Storyteller 5:	Two shoes that don't even match! A painful sight. Terrible. Crusoe's been lucky, but he must be sad to lose his friends.
Storyteller 1:	Of course. And with night coming on, he believes he's fair game for any hungry beasts that prowl in the night.
Storyteller 5:	What can he do? Climb a tree? Were there any trees?
Daniel Defoe:	Good thought. As luck would have it, he does find a tree.

Robinson Crusoe: A thick bushy tree, like a fir, but thorny . . . where I resolved to sit all night—and consider the next day what death I should die, for as yet I saw no prospect of life.

Storyteller 1: But he is not defeated! He begins to salvage everything he can from the wrecked ship.

Storyteller 2: And this was not an easy job. Mr. Defoe knows this.

Storyteller 1: But Crusoe does what he has to do. He swims out to the ship and constructs a raft. Then he begins to float food, clothes, chests, tools, guns, and ammunition back to the shore.

Storyteller 5: You might as well take it all, buddy. Everyone else is drowned.

Storyteller 1: Crusoe makes more than twelve trips before the wrecked ship finally goes under. He salvages as much as he can—supplies, hopefully, for his survival. But he's not secure yet.

Robinson Crusoe: My next work was to view the country, and seek a proper place for my habitation, and where to stow my goods, to secure them from whatever might happen.

Storyteller 2: First, he barricades himself with the chests and boards he's brought on shore. Then he makes a tent with sails from the ship. And he piles up everything he's salvaged all around the tent. He works hard to keep out any savage beasts or men.

Storyteller 1: He doesn't know yet there are no savage beasts. But strange men will be a different problem.

Storyteller 5: I think you're talking about—the cannibals.

Storyteller 1: He knows nothing about the cannibals—yet. Worst thing of all, he doesn't know he's completely alone—for now.

Storyteller 5: Does Robinson Crusoe stay there—in that tent?

Storyteller 2: Well, before long, he sets out to roam about the island for a better site, a more permanent one.

Storyteller 5: I think Crusoe must have itchy feet, too.

Storyteller 3: Right. Mr. Defoe knew what it meant to go exploring. He gave Robinson Crusoe that same urge, that same curiosity.

Storyteller 5: But I think Robinson Crusoe is a practical man, too. He seems to know a lot—about what to do and how to do it.

Storyteller 3: Well, his author grew up being practical. Plus, he studied hard. He learned a lot. Correct, Mr. Defoe?

Daniel Defoe: My teachers insisted upon such work. They taught me to write good, clear English, and of course I studied history, geography, natural science, and astronomy.

Storyteller 5: Whew. That's a ton of homework! You survived all that?

Daniel Defoe: Ah, well, to survive, my friend, one has to be practical, to work hard, and to evaluate one's position—like Crusoe does:

Robinson Crusoe: I drew up my state of affairs in writing . . . and I stated very impartially . . . the *comforts* I enjoyed against the *miseries* I suffered. I labeled these opposites the Good and the Evil. Thus: I am cast upon a horrible desolate island, void of all hope of recovery. *But* I am alive; and not drowned, as all my ship's company were. *(Pause)* Yet, I am singled out and separated, as it were, from all the world, to be miserable. *But* I am singled out too from all the ship's crew, to be spared from death; and He that miraculously saved me from death, can deliver me from this condition. *(Pause)* Still, I am divided from mankind, a solitaire. . . . *But* I am not starved, and perishing in a barren place, affording no sustenance. *(Pause)* I have no clothes to cover me. *But* I am in a hot climate, where, if I had clothes, I could hardly wear them. *(Pause)* I am without any . . . means to resist any violence of man or beast. *But* I am cast on an island where I see no wild beast to hurt me. *(Pause)* I have no soul to speak to. *But* God wonderfully sent the ship in near enough to the shore, that I have got out so many necessary things, as will . . . enable me to supply myself, even as long as I live.

Storyteller 3: So Robinson Crusoe thanks his God and trusts his God. That's not very surprising. Mr. Defoe was a religious man. Isn't that right, sir?

Daniel Defoe: Indeed. I grew up steeped in religion. My father expected me to become a Presbyterian clergyman. I rebelled against that. Not too surprising. My parents were religious rebels—Dissenters, like the Puritans who landed on Plymouth Rock in America.

Storyteller 1: Weren't religious dissenters punished in England?

Daniel Defoe: Indeed. It was illegal to worship our way. So I wrote a paper trying to show how those laws were unfair. Then I published it.

Storyteller 2: That was pretty dangerous. What happened to you?

Daniel Defoe: They pilloried me as punishment.

Storyteller 5: I've read about that—women accused of being witches were pilloried back in Salem, Massachusetts. But what *is* a pillory?

Daniel Defoe: It's a wooden frame with holes for your head and hands. They locked prisoners in that frame, then put them on display before everybody.

Storyteller 5: How embarrassing! How did your public react?

Storyteller 3: Ordinary people admired Defoe for what he wrote. They didn't ridicule him. They brought him flowers. He became a hero, even when they sentenced him to Newgate Prison for two years.

Storyteller 5: That must have been a powerful paper he wrote.

Storyteller 3: It was. He had a powerful pen. A practical pen.

Daniel Defoe: It was useful. It earned me money that I sorely needed to provide for my wife and children. Besides, I received pleasure attacking unfair laws, the lack of jobs, and the treatment of poor people. We needed more education in England, better trade, the establishment of Savings Banks.

Storyteller 1: Savings Banks? Ah, didn't you have trouble with money, sir?

Daniel Defoe: Yes. Twice I lost everything, went bankrupt.

Storyteller 3: But he always repaid his debts.

Storyteller 2: This is ironic. In the novel, Crusoe finds plenty of money on the shipwrecked ship. He takes it all, but he has no way to spend it—nothing to buy. Money doesn't mean survival for him.

Storyteller 3:	But money meant survival for Defoe and his family. He often wrote for money.
Storyteller 5:	Is that why he wrote *Robinson Crusoe*?
Storyteller 4:	Maybe. He was in his late fifties when he wrote this novel. That's an old man for the eighteenth century. Most people died at thirty-five or forty in those days. But maybe after all the years of serious writing, Mr. Defoe wanted to entertain his readers—inspire them—horrors and all.
Storyteller 5:	Horrors and all? Are we back to the cannibals?
Storyteller 3:	We are. Time passes. Crusoe's been alone on that island for sixteen years. But listen to what he wrote in *his* diary:
Robinson Crusoe:	It happened one day, about noon. Going towards my boat, I was exceedingly surprised with the print of a man's naked foot on the shore, which was very plain to be seen in the sand. I stood like one thunderstruck, or as if I had seen an apparition: I listened, I looked round me, but I could hear nothing, nor see anything. . . . I went up the shore and down the shore, but it was all one; I could see no other impression but that one.
Storyteller 5:	He finds no one? No other footprints? Nothing?
Storyteller 2:	Not then—not until two years later. But now he does realize how easy it would be for savages to land on his island, whether by mistake or on purpose.
Storyteller 5:	But the cannibals. Do they land? Does he see them again?
Storyteller 1:	Well, one day he thinks he sees a boat, perhaps, far out at sea.
Storyteller 2:	Curious and fearful, he explores a corner of the island he's never seen before. *That's* when he finds something terrible.
Robinson Crusoe:	I was perfectly confounded and amazed; nor is it possible for me to express the horror of my mind, at seeing the shore spread with skulls, hands, feet, and other bones of human bodies; and, particularly, I observed a place where there had been a fire made, and a circle dug in the earth, like a cockpit, where I supposed the savage wretches had sat down to their inhuman feastings upon the bodies of their fellow-creatures.
Storyteller 5:	Wow. Enough of the gory details.
Storyteller 1:	It affects you? Listen to Robinson Crusoe and *his* reaction:
Robinson Crusoe:	I turned away from the horrid spectacle; my stomach grew sick, and I was just at the point of fainting, when nature discharged the disorder from my stomach.
Storyteller 3:	Oh, Mr. Defoe, you did a good job describing that!
Robinson Crusoe:	Having vomited with uncommon violence, I was a little relieved, but could not bear to stay in the place a moment; so I got me up the hill again with all the speed I could, and walked on towards my own habitation.
Storyteller 5:	Okay. Is that the end of the cannibal thing?
Storyteller 1:	I thought you wanted it all. There's more. Time passes. Now Crusoe's been on the island for nearly twenty-five years.
Storyteller 5:	So Crusoe's how old now? In his fifties? Not too old, I guess.
Storyteller 3:	Remember, a man in his fifties in those years was an old man.

Storyteller 5:	So Mr. Defoe, in his fifties and an old man, is writing this book about Robinson Crusoe, who's an old man, too, in his fifties.
Storyteller 1:	Old, yes, but Robinson Crusoe is surviving, ready and able to take on whatever threatens him.
Storyteller 3:	Like our author, Mr. Defoe, who goes on to write more novels!
Storyteller 5:	More novels, but without cannibals I hope?
Storyteller 4:	That's correct—but they are novels of adventure.
Storyteller 5:	Are these novels without savages?
Daniel Defoe:	Savages? Well, I must admit that in my day we often called the natives of newly discovered lands savages, whether they were cannibals or not. In general, we feared these natives. But sometimes we called them Noble Savages.
Storyteller 1:	Robinson Crusoe thinks these savages are anything but noble. He fears them. He continues to prepare for the worst, the very worst—being invaded by these unknown natives.
Storyteller 5:	And the very worst happens, doesn't it? Do tell!
Robinson Crusoe:	I was surprised, one morning early, with seeing no less than five canoes all on shore together on my side the island, and the people who belonged to them all landed, and out of my sight.
Storyteller 2:	So he climbs a nearby hill, and keeping well hidden, raises his spyglass to see at least thirty men below him on the shore.
Robinson Crusoe:	I observed, by the help of my perspective glass, that they had a fire kindled, and that they had meat dressed. How they had cooked it I knew not, or what it was; but they were all dancing, in I know not how many barbarous gestures and figures, round the fire.
Storyteller 1:	Then he sees the savages drag two men from the boats. The captives stagger to their feet. The savages knock down one of the men, and immediately—
Robinson Crusoe:	Two or three others . . . were cutting him open for their cookery, while the other victim is left standing by himself, till they should be ready for him.
Storyteller 5:	Here's his chance! Does the savage make a run for it—escape?
Robinson Crusoe:	He started away from them, and ran with incredible swiftness along the sands, directly towards me.
Storyteller 1:	But three men are after him. He dashes on, until he comes to the creek. The tide is up and the creek full. He plunges in. The others are close behind, but he swims across the creek with amazing strength.
Robinson Crusoe:	When the three persons came to the creek, I found that two of them could swim, but the third . . . went no farther. The two who swam were yet more than twice as long swimming over the creek as the fellow who fled from them. It came very warmly upon my thoughts, and indeed irresistibly, that now was the time to get me a servant, and perhaps a companion or assistant, and that I was called plainly by Providence to save this poor creature's life.
Storyteller 5:	I'd think Crusoe would want to get away—go back to his fort or his cave. Those are cannibals!

Storyteller 4:	Mr. Defoe did not write about a scaredy-cat, you know. Wait!
Robinson Crusoe:	I placed myself in the way between the pursuers and the pursued, hallowing aloud to him that fled, who, looking back, was at first perhaps as much frightened at me as at them; but I beckon'd with my hand to him to come back; and in the meantime, I slowly advanced towards the two that followed: then rushing at once upon the foremost, I knock'd him down with the stock of my piece.
Storyteller 2:	Good work! And remember, beside his guns, Crusoe has knives and a great sword.
Storyteller 1:	But he's afraid to shoot his guns. The gunsmoke and the sound might alert the savages back at that terrible feast.
Robinson Crusoe:	At that distance, it would not have been easily heard, and being out of sight of the smoke too, they would not have easily known what to make of it.
Storyteller 2:	Good thinking, Crusoe!
Robinson Crusoe:	Having knock'd this fellow down, the other who pursu'd with him stopp'd, as if he had been frightened; and I advanced apace towards him: but as I came nearer, I perceived presently that he had a bow and arrow, and was fitting it to shoot at me.
Storyteller 5:	Big trouble! He's about to be killed!
Robinson Crusoe:	I was then necessitated to shoot at him first, which I did, and killed him at the first shot; the poor savage who fled, had stopped; though he saw both his enemies fallen, and killed, as he thought; yet was so frighted with the fire, and noise of my piece; that he stood stock still. . . . I hollow'd again to him. . . . at length he came close to me, and then kneel'd down, kiss'd the ground, and laid his head upon the ground, and taking me by the foot, set my foot upon his head. . . . this it seems was in token of swearing to be my slave for ever.
Storyteller 5:	So far so good. But is that first savage really dead?
Robinson Crusoe:	The savage who I knocked down, was not kill'd, but stunn'd with the blow. I pointed to him . . . showing my savage the man was not dead; upon this my savage spoke some words to me, and though I could not understand them, yet I thought they were pleasant to hear, for they were the first sound of a man's voice that I had heard, *my own excepted*, for above twenty-five years.
Storyteller 5:	But what about that first savage—the one that's still alive on the ground?
Robinson Crusoe:	I perceived that my savage began to be afraid; but when I saw that, I presented my other piece at the man, as if I would shoot him; upon this my savage, for so I call him now, made a motion to me to lend him my sword which hung naked in a belt by my side—which I did. He no sooner had it, but he runs to his enemy, and at one blow, cut off his head.
Storyteller 5:	Cut off his head? Cut it off with one blow?
Robinson Crusoe:	When he had done this, he comes laughing to me in sign of triumph, and brought me the sword again, and with abundance of gestures which I did not understand, laid it down *(Pause)* with the head of the savage, that he had kill'd just before me.
Storyteller 5:	A bloodthirsty scene! Can Crusoe trust him?
Storyteller 2:	Sounds like he's happy to have found a companion. Look what Crusoe does:

Robinson Crusoe: I carry'd him, not to my castle, but quite away to my cave, on the farthest part of the island. . . . Here I gave him bread, and a bunch of raisins to eat, and a draught of water, which I found he was indeed in great distress for, by his running; and having refreshed him, I made signs for him to go lie down and sleep; pointing to a place where I had laid a great parcel of rice straw, and a blanket upon it, which I used to sleep upon myself sometimes, so the poor creature laid down, and went to sleep.

Storyteller 5: He *is* trusting him—as if he were a true friend.

Robinson Crusoe: I understood him in many things, and let him know, I was very well pleased with him; in a little time I began to speak to him and teach him to speak to me; and first, I made him know his name should be *Friday*, which was the day I saved his life; I called him so for the memory of the time.

Storyteller 5: I'm sorry. I'm still uneasy—the way that man can use a sword. *And* a bow and arrow. Can Robinson Crusoe really trust him? The man's a cannibal—a *savage*! What happens next?

Daniel Defoe: Stop! Stop! Desist! Do not give away the ending! *(Pause)* Actually, my young friends, I'm sure you can find a copy of my novel at your local bookseller for very few coins.

Announcer: *(Enters to center stage)* Or you can check out a copy at your library—*Robinson Crusoe*.

Daniel Defoe: Let me give the entire title, should you desire to purchase my book. I call it, "The Life and Strange Surprizing Adventures of Robinson Crusoe, of York Mariner: Who lived Eight and Twenty Years, all alone in an un-inhabited Island on the Coast of America, near the Mouth of the Great River of Oroonoque; Having been cast on Shore by Shipwreck, wherein all the Men perished but himself. With An Account how he was at last as strangely deliver'd by Pyrates."

Announcer: Or you can find it under Defoe, Daniel. *Robinson Crusoe*, by Daniel Defoe, the story of one extraordinary survivor, told by another. *(Announcer shows book title, then bows and exits)*

The Class Act of Charles Dickens
and *Great Expectations*

A great divide separated the upper and lower classes during the nineteenth century in Great Britain. In 1837, when Queen Victoria assumed the throne at the age of eighteen, she faced an industrial revolution and the great expectations of her people.

In 1837, Charles Dickens was twenty-five and already dramatizing the aspirations and inequalities of the lower classes to an admiring public in England and abroad.

In this Victorian Age, marked by hopes and disappointments, Dickens fought for the reform of class disparities in argumentative articles and essays. But when he turned to writing novels, he touched the heart and the imagination of his readers. In novels such as *David Copperfield* and *Oliver Twist* we understand and empathize with the lower class. In *Great Expectations* our insight grows with the rise and fall of Pip, the boy—the man.

Dickens did not emerge from a privileged background like Queen Victoria. He began life as the son of a government clerk, a life that seemed comfortable enough until the family fortunes sank. Debtor's prison claimed the father, and work in a bootblacking factory introduced twelve-year-old Charles Dickens to poverty and oppression.

Always a great reader, a watcher, and a listener, Dickens's love for the theatre led him into acting, producing, lecturing, and performing throughout England, in Italy, and in America. His extraordinary memories of landscapes, rooms, clothes, faces, names, and voices brighten every scene, every story he created.

While working on yet another novel, Dickens died on June 9, 1870, at the age of fifty-eight—the born storyteller of fifteen novels, classics all—like *Great Expectations*.

The Victorian Age, better for the influence of this classic author Charles Dickens, ended with the queen's death in 1901.

Presentation of Charles Dickens Script

Trying to read the mind and psyche of Charles Dickens, the most famous author of the Victorian Age, leads us into the pathways that he traveled and the journeys that he gave his characters.

Dickens was dramatic about his life, throughout his life. This script touches on the memorable past that influenced Dickens and demonstrates how he interwove his own life with his imaginary worlds.

The readers theatre script calls for fourteen readers. Casting suggestions are as follows:

Boys: Dickens, Pip, Storytellers 1 and 2, Joe, Jagger, and Convict.

Girls: Estella, Miss Havisham, and Biddy.

Either boys or girls can be cast as Storytellers 3, 4, 5, and the Announcer.

Stage Props

13 reading stands, if possible

13 tall stools or chairs

Hand Props

14 scripts (plus 1 for the teacher)

14 black folders for scripts

1 copy of *Great Expectations* for Announcer to show title at the end of the show

The Class Act of Charles Dickens and *Great Expectations*

Production note: Storytellers 1–5 and Dickens and Pip placed as noted. Other characters: Estella, 6; Miss Havisham, 7; Biddy, 8; Joe, 9; Jaggers, 10; Convict, 11

```
        X X X              X X X
        3 4 5              6 7 8


    X            X X X    X X X
 Dickens         1 Pip 2  9 10 11

            Announcer
```

—◄◈►—

Announcer:	*(Steps to center stage)* Welcome to Storyteller Theatre—where today we will play out the extraordinary career and writings of Charles Dickens. *(Pause)* That was a little pun, folks. Theatre? Play out? *(Pause)* Okay, you'll see—for Charles Dickens is dramatic! Full of dreams! Full of disappointments—but great expectations.
Storyteller 3:	I get it!—the name of the book. It's *Great Expectations*.
Storyteller 5:	We were expecting that!
Storyteller 1:	Yes, we were, weren't we, Mr. Dickens?
Dickens:	Well, I wasn't, but carry on.
Announcer:	*(Bows to Dickens)* But, of course, Mr. Dickens. It's you, the classic storyteller, whom we honor today—you and your novel. Indeed, we shall carry on! Curtain rises, and I shall make my exit. *(Exits)*
Storyteller 4:	I don't know this book. I haven't a clue. Who's in it?
Storyteller 1:	A great cast. Mr. Pumblechook, Orlick, and Wemmick, Trabb, Jagger, and Startop *(Faster)* Magwitch, Pocket, Flopson, and Biddy.
Storyteller 2:	Not to mention Mr. Wopsle and Joe and Mrs. Joe.
Storyteller 1:	Or Miss Havisham, Estella—and our hero, Pip!
Storyteller 4:	You say Pip? What kind of a name is that? Pip!
Dickens:	A simple name for a simple lad—at least, simple at the beginning.
Pip:	I have the book. Let me read Pip.
Storyteller 2:	And we have the book. We'll help!
Storyteller 1:	We will. And we'll start at the beginning. *(Nods at Pip)* Pip?
Pip:	My father's family name being Pirrip, and my Christian name Philip, my infant tongue could make of both names nothing longer or more explicit than Pip. So I called myself Pip, and came to be called Pip.
Storyteller 3:	Logical choice. Obviously Philip Pirrip is a tongue-twister.

Storyteller 4:	He named himself? Sounds like he might be an orphan.
Dickens:	He is, and he never knew his parents. He lives with his married sister and her husband, Joe, a blacksmith. Pip is small—only seven years old in the beginning— and he has small hopes.
Storyteller 4:	But as he grows older, I bet he expects something better.
Storyteller 5:	Dare I say it? Great expectations? Where does our drama begin?
Dickens:	In England, of course. In a graveyard—when, out of the mist, an escaped convict appears. But enough from me. Let Pip tell you:
Pip:	Ours was the marsh country, down by the river, within, as the river wound, twenty miles of the sea.
Storyteller 1:	And that dark flat wilderness beyond the churchyard, intersected with dikes and mounds and gates, with scattered cattle feeding on it, was the marshes; and that low leaden line beyond was the river;
Storyteller 2:	And that distant savage lair from which the wind was rushing was the sea; and that small bundle of shivers growing afraid of it all—
Pip:	And beginning to *cry* was *me*, Pip!
Convict:	Hold your noise!
Storyteller 2:	A man started up from among the graves at the side of the church porch.
Convict:	Keep still you little devil, or I'll cut your throat!
Storyteller 1:	A fearful man, all in coarse gray, with a great iron on his leg. A man with no hat, and with broken shoes, and with an old rag tied round his head. A man who had been soaked in water—
Storyteller 2:	And smothered in mud, and lamed by stones, and cut by flints, and stung by nettles, and torn by briers;
Storyteller 1:	Who limped, and shivered, and glared, and growled;
Pip:	And whose teeth chattered in his head as he seized me by the chin. Oh! Don't cut my throat, sir. Pray don't do it sir.
Convict:	Now, lookee here, the question being whether you're to be let to live. You know what a file is?
Pip:	Yes, sir.
Convict:	You get me a file. And you get me wittles. . . . Do it.
Pip:	Yes, sir.
Convict:	You do it, and you never dare to say a word or dare to make a sign concerning your having seen such a person as me, or any person sumever, and you shall be let to live. You fail . . . and your liver shall be tore out, roasted and ate.
Pip:	Yes, sir. I saw him go. . . . On the edge of the river I could make out the only two black things.
Storyteller l:	One was the beacon by which the sailors steered;
Storyteller 2:	The other a gibbet with some chains hanging to it, which had once held a pirate. The man was limping on toward this latter, as if—

Pip:	*(Slowly)* As if he were the pirate come to life, and come down, and going back to hook himself up again.
Storyteller 3:	Curtain! End of Chapter One—and printed first in serial form!
Storyteller 5:	No wonder people took to the streets at this point. They were yelling for the next chapter. That first part gives me the chills!
Storyteller 4:	Who is this man? Why is he wearing chains?
Dickens:	He comes from a prison ship—one of the Hulks—derelict ships, anchored in the Thames River and made into prisons. As a boy, I could see the Hulks from my home on the marshlands. Occasionally, convicts did escape from them, but not for long.
Storyteller 5:	Hunted down—and returned to the ships?
Dickens:	Or they were hanged on the gibbet.
Storyteller 4:	Punished by hanging—dead or alive on the gallows!
Storyteller 5:	You'd think Pip would want to leave such a depressing place, especially after he meets the girl, Estella. Remember?
Storyteller 3:	*(Dreamily)* I do like that name *(slowly)* Estella—beautiful, starlike.
Storyteller 4:	Stars glow in the distance. They're beautiful, but cold and hard.
Dickens:	Like Estella—beautiful but caustic—a puzzle to Pip. Estella lives with and, you could say, serves Miss Havisham.
Pip:	I had heard of Miss Havisham up town.
Storyteller 2:	Everybody for miles round had heard of Miss Havisham up town—as an immensely rich and grim lady who lived in a large and dismal house barricaded against robbers, and who led a life of seclusion.
Pip:	Miss Havisham sent for me and paid me to play there, to entertain her. But it was Estella who let me in that big house. One day—
Storyteller l:	As we were going with our candle along the dark passage, Estella stopped all of a sudden, and facing round, said in her taunting manner, with her face quite close to mine:
Estella:	Well?
Pip:	Well, miss?
Storyteller 2:	She stood looking at me, and of course I stood looking at her.
Estella:	Am I pretty?
Pip:	Yes, I think you are very pretty.
Estella:	Am I insulting?
Pip:	Not so much so as you were last time.
Estella:	Not so much so?
Pip:	No.
Storyteller 1:	She fired when she asked the last question, and she slapped my face with such force as she had, when I answered it.
Estella:	Now? You little coarse monster, what do you think of me now?

Pip: I shall not tell you.

Estella: Because you are going to tell Miss Havisham upstairs. Is that it?

Pip: No, that's not it.

Estella: Why don't you cry again, you little wretch?

Pip: Because I'll never cry for you again.

Storyteller 2: Which was, I suppose, as false a declaration as ever was made;

Pip: I was crying for her then, and I know what I know of the pain she cost me afterwards. . . . She was dreadfully proud. . . . She had said I was common. . . . I knew I was common, and . . . I wished I was not common.

Storyteller 4: You're right. Estella may be pretty, but she's brittle—hard inside.

Storyteller 5: Miss Havisham must have something to do with that.

Dickens: Remember, Miss Havisham pays Pip to entertain her at her house. Pip finds Miss Havisham very bizarre on his very first visit:

Pip: In an arm-chair, with an elbow resting on the table and her head leaning on that hand, sat the strangest lady I have ever seen, or shall ever see.

Storyteller 1: She was dressed in rich materials—satins and lace and silks—all of white. Her shoes were white. And she had a long, white veil dependent from her hair, and she had bridal flowers in her hair—

Storyteller 2: But her hair was white.

Pip: Everything within my view which ought to be white had been white long ago, and had lost its luster, and was faded and yellow. I saw that the bride within the bridal dress had withered like the dress . . . and that the figure on which it now hung loose had shrunk to skin and bone. Then the old lady at the table spoke:

Miss Havisham: Who is it?

Pip: Pip, ma'am. Come to play.

Miss Havisham: Come nearer; let me look at you. Come close.

Storyteller 1: It was when I stood before her, avoiding her eyes, that I took note of the surrounding objects in detail, and saw that her watch had stopped at twenty minutes to nine, and that a clock in the room had stopped at twenty minutes to nine.

Miss Havisham: Look at me. You are not afraid of a woman who has never seen the sun since you were born?

Pip: I regret to state that I was not afraid of telling the enormous lie comprehended in the answer No.

Miss Havisham: Do you know what I touch here?

Storyteller 2: And she laid her hands, one upon the other, on her left side.

Pip: Yes, ma'am.

Miss Havisham: What do I touch?

Pip: Your heart.

Miss Havisham: Broken! Broken!

Storyteller 1:	She uttered the word with an eager look, and with strong emphasis, and with a weird smile that had a kind of boast in it.
Storyteller 4:	That's pretty horrible—spooky. She sounds like death.
Dickens:	*(Sighs)* She dies an unnatural death, to be sure. But you see, in my time, even early death was everywhere—in the homes, the schools, the prisons, on the streets.
Storyteller 5:	And did death touch you personally?
Dickens:	Every death touches us in some way. But yes, when I was two years old, my baby brother died. Death touched me then.
Storyteller 3:	And you were deeply touched by that death—even at two?
Dickens:	I remember it still. Then when I was ten, my sister Harriet died. Later, my beautiful sister-in-law, Mary, died—*(Pause)* too soon. Too soon. But nothing matched the death of my baby daughter.
Storyteller 3:	Deaths happen in your novels—in *Great Expectations*.
Dickens:	Deaths happen in life. I don't deny I have a fear of death. Perhaps we all do. *(Pause)* In any case, Miss Havisham is frightening, but Pip is bewitched by Estella. That night Pip can hardly sleep:
Pip:	I thought long after I laid me down how common Estella would consider Joe, a mere blacksmith: how thick his boots, and how coarse his hands.
Storyteller 1:	I thought how Joe and my sister were then sitting in the kitchen, and how I had come up to bed from the kitchen, and how Miss Havisham and Estella never sat in a kitchen, but were far above the level of such common things.
Pip:	That was a memorable day to me, for it made great changes in me.
Storyteller 2:	But it is the same with any life.
Dickens:	Imagine one selected day struck out of it, and think how different its course would have been . . . but for the formation of the first link on one memorable day.
Storyteller 4:	Are we speaking of Fate with a capital F?
Storyteller 3:	We're speaking of a turning point in Pip's life. He's growing up, and longs to be somebody else. He has aspirations.
Storyteller 4:	Well, wishing won't make it so. We all know that.
Dickens:	True. Pip has no way to make changes happen in his life. He must follow the path laid out for him—to work, to be a blacksmith's apprentice to Joe, his brother-in-law.
Storyteller 4:	Apprentice to a blacksmith? But Pip's only a boy!
Dickens:	Matters not a whit. Pip lives in the nineteenth century—think 1850. The Industrial Revolution is barely underway. Poor children in the lower classes, children like Pip, have no choice but to work—some went to work as early as four or five.
Storyteller 5:	Personal experience, Mr. Dickens?
Dickens:	A bitter experience. At the age of twelve I was put to work in a blacking factory.

Storyteller 3:	Hold on. Joe sees that factory in London later on—when he pays a visit to Pip and chats about the sights he's seen.
Joe:	Why, yes, sir, me and Wopsle went off straight to look at the Blacking Ware'us.
Storyteller 5:	I guess I don't know what that is. A blacking warehouse?
Dickens:	No, I don't suppose you would—it's a concern, a factory, that made polish for blacking the boots of gentlemen.
Storyteller 4:	And you, too, worked there as a kid? I thought your father was well-off. I didn't know your family was poor.
Dickens:	We weren't—in the beginning. My father was a clerk in service for the Navy, a paymaster, you might say. We lived well enough, near Portsmouth in the south, then Chatham in the north—near the marshlands.
Storyteller 3:	Then poor? Something really, really bad must have happened.
Dickens:	Devastating—to me. My father handled money. He paid the naval workmen. He paid the crews on the ships. *(Pause)* He couldn't handle his own money.
Storyteller 4:	I get it. He went into debt.
Dickens:	And was sent thence into Debtor's Prison and poverty—and I to the blacking factory, working ten hours a day fixing labels onto jars of blacking for gentlemen.
Storyteller 3:	It's still in your memory, isn't it?—the poverty, the work.
Dickens:	I don't like to talk about it! I don't like to think about it—the stink, the woodworm, the rats. My whole nature was so penetrated with the grief and humiliation of such considerations, that even now, famous and caressed and happy, I often forget in my dreams that I have a dear wife and children; even that I am a man; and wander desolately back to that time of my life.
Storyteller 3:	Pip is unhappy, dissatisfied with his life, too. He confesses some of his hopes and aspirations to Biddy, his tutor and close friend:
Pip:	Biddy, I want to be a gentleman.
Biddy:	Oh, I wouldn't, if I was you! I don't think it would answer.
Pip:	Biddy, I have particular reasons for wanting to be a gentleman.
Biddy:	You know best, Pip, but don't you think you're happier as you are?
Pip:	Biddy, I am not at all happy as I am. I'm disgusted with my calling and my life. . . . but what would it signify to me, being *coarse* and *common*, if nobody had told me so!
Biddy:	It was neither a very true nor a very polite thing to say. . . . Who said it?
Pip:	The beautiful young lady at Miss Havisham's, and she's more beautiful than any body ever was, and I admire her dreadfully, and I want to be a gentleman on her account.
Biddy:	Do you want to be a gentleman, to spite her or to win her over?
Pip:	I don't know.
Dickens:	There you have it—aspirations. Longings. Often that's the end of it—unless something or someone steps in.

Storyteller 3:	Unless Fate steps in.
Dickens:	Or maybe we, ourselves, take some action that will change us.
Storyteller 3:	Pip becomes a great reader. Did you?
Dickens:	*(Slight laugh)* I read everything I could put my hands on. I read for the law. I studied journalism. I became a reporter. All the while, stories ran through my mind.
Storyteller 5:	And with all this work, what did *you* long for?
Dickens:	In particular, Gad's Hill. My father took me on a walk near our home. We passed a big house called Gad's Hill. I thought it was a mansion, and I wanted to live there. My father . . . said, If you were to be persevering and were to work hard, you might some day come to live in it.
Storyteller 5:	And you did come to live in it?
Dickens:	I did—some thirty years later—I and my wife, Catherine, and our children. *(Smiles)* All in all, we had ten children.
Storyteller 4:	Ten children? You did need a big house for ten kids!
Storyteller 3:	So—you persevered, wrote fourteen novels along the way, and finally bought your dream house.
Storyteller 5:	How about those lecture trips to America? All those performances! You toured the entire country giving readings.
Storyteller 4:	I don't think we can call that hard work. I bet you loved that, Mr. Dickens.
Dickens:	The traveling—the performing? I did love it. I often thought I should have been an actor instead of a writer.
Storyteller 5:	You loved the stage?
Dickens:	Indeed! I saw every play I could. We put on amateur performances of our own. I loved the excitement of the theatre, the inventions of lights and scenery and costumes.
Storyteller 4:	Aha. That explains your love for bright, fancy clothes. They're really your costumes!
Dickens:	*(Momentarily examines fancy vest)* Perhaps that is so. Perhaps.
Storyteller 4:	And the actors? How about the actresses?
Dickens:	*(Smiles)* Many members of the theater companies became my friends—the ladies as well.
Storyteller 3:	*(Pause. Eyebrows up)* Shall we move on? Speaking of being theatrical—how about those descriptions of Pip's friends and acquaintances? They seem typecast for every role. Example?
Storyteller 1:	Uncle Pumblechook; a large, hard-breathing, middle-aged, slow man, with a mouth like a fish, dull, staring eyes, and sandy hair standing upright on his head, so that he looked as if he had just been all but choked, and had that moment come to.
Storyteller 5:	Don't forget Mr. Wopsle. He, too, has aspirations and longings.
Storyteller 2:	Mr. Wopsle, united to a Roman nose and a large shining bald forehead, had a deep voice which he was uncommonly proud of.

Storyteller 3:	He becomes an actor! Tell about Mr. Wemmick, with such a post-office of a mouth that he had a mechanical appearance of smiling.
Storyteller 1:	Mechanical, even when he eats.
Pip:	Wemmick was at his desk, lunching—and crunching—on a dry, hard biscuit; pieces of which he threw from time to time into his slit of a mouth, as if he were posting them.
Storyteller 3:	Like a letter? You know, some scenes can be funny *and* awful.
Storyteller 5:	Like that scene when Mrs. Joe cleans Pip up.
Pip:	She pounced on me, like an eagle on a lamb, and my face was squeezed into wooden bowls in sinks, and my head was put under taps of water-butts, and I was soaped, and kneaded, and toweled, and thumped, and harrowed, and rasped, until I really was quite beside myself.
Storyteller 3:	So she's cleaning him up. Does that set him on the road to becoming a gentleman?
Dickens:	Not exactly. Such changes require time. But Pip does grow up.
Storyteller 5:	Is he any better off? Is he getting anywhere?
Dickens:	He remains an apprentice to Joe, the blacksmith, for four years. Then, one night at the inn of The Three Jolly Bargemen, a man appears that nobody knows.
Pip:	The strange gentleman, with an air of authority not to be disputed, and with a manner expressive of knowing something secret about every one of us . . . remained standing: his left hand in his pocket, and he biting the forefinger of his right. Looking round at us, as we all quailed before him, he began to speak:
Jaggers:	From information I have received, I have reason to believe there is a blacksmith among you by the name Joseph—or Joe—Gargery. Which is the man?
Joe:	Here is the man.
Storyteller 2:	The strange gentleman beckoned him out of his place, and Joe went.
Jaggers:	You have an apprentice, commonly known as Pip? Is he here?
Pip:	I am here! The stranger did not recognize me, but I recognized him as the gentleman I had met on the stairs, on the occasion of my second visit to Miss Havisham.
Storyteller 1:	I checked off again in detail his large head, his dark complexion, his deep-set eyes, his bushy black eyebrows, his large watch-chain, his strong black dots of beard and whisker, and even the smell of scented soap on his great hand.
Jaggers:	I wish to have a private conference with you two. . . . It will take a little time. Perhaps we had better go to your place of residence.
Storyteller 2:	Amidst a wondering silence, we three walked out of The Jolly Bargemen, and in a wondering silence walked home. . . . Our conference was held in the state parlor, which was feebly lighted by one candle.
Jaggers:	My name is Jaggers, and I am a lawyer in London. I am pretty well known. I have unusual business to transact with you, and I commence by explaining that it is not of my originating. . . . What I have to do as the confidential agent of another, I do. No less, no more.
Storyteller 2:	He then went on:

Jaggers:	Now, Joseph Gargery, I am the bearer of an offer to relieve you of this young fellow, your apprentice. You would not object to cancel his indentures at his request and for his good? You would want nothing for so doing?
Joe:	Lord forbid that I should want any thing for not standing in Pip's way.
Jaggers:	Lord forbidding is pious, but not to the purpose. The question is, would you want any thing? Do you want any thing?
Joe:	The answer is, No.
Jaggers:	Very well. Recollect the admission you have made, and don't try to go from it presently.
Joe:	Who's agoing to try?
Jaggers:	I don't say any body is. . . . Now I return to this young fellow. And the communication I have got to make is, that he has Great Expectations.
Storyteller 4:	Joe and I gasped, and looked at one another.
Jaggers:	I am instructed to communicate to him that he will come into a handsome property. Further, that it is the desire of the present possessor of that property that he be immediately removed from his present sphere of life and from this place, and be brought up as a gentleman—in a word, as a young fellow of great expectations.
Pip:	My dream was out.
Storyteller 1:	My wild fancy was surpassed by sober reality.
Storyteller 2:	Miss Havisham was going to make my fortune on a grand scale.
Jaggers:	Now, Mr. Pip, you are to understand that the name of the person who is your liberal benefactor remains a profound secret until the person chooses to reveal it. . . . When or where that intention may be carried out, I can not say; no one can say. It may be years. . . . The person from whom you derive your expectations, and the secret is solely held by that person and me.
Storyteller 4:	It's a mystery, I know it! It has to be that lady, Miss Havisham!
Dickens:	Is it? Does it have to be? Well, you may be right. On the other hand, you may be wrong. Pip has many adventures in my book.
Storyteller 4:	It's all very well to wave a magic wand and announce great expectations for Pip, but what about money? He'll need money.
Dickens:	Patience, friend, patience. Listen to Lawyer Jaggers:
Jaggers:	Although I use the term *expectations* more than once, you are not endowed with expectations only. There is already lodged in my hands a sum of money amply sufficient for your suitable education and maintenance.
Storyteller 5:	Whew! Money! That's a relief.
Jaggers:	It is considered that you must be better educated . . . and that you will be alive to the importance and necessity of at once entering on that advantage.
Pip:	I had always longed for it.
Jaggers:	Never mind what you've always longed for, Mr. Pip. Keep to the record. If you long for it now, that's enough. Am I answered that you are ready to be placed at once under some proper tutor?

Pip:	Yes.
Jaggers:	When will you come to London?
Storyteller l:	I said . . . I supposed I could come directly.
Dickens:	Pip's situation is changing, and he knows it. That night, his excitement fades as he looks ahead and begins to worry.
Pip:	I put my light out, and crept into bed; and it was an uneasy bed now, and I never slept the old sound sleep in it any more.
Announcer:	*(Enters to center stage)* Curtain! Be careful what you wish for, right? Pip's climb from the lower class to the gentleman class is full of success, but disappointments, too. Want to solve the mystery? Learn the secret? *(Holds up copy of novel)* It's dramatized in this book by Charles Dickens—*Great Expectations*. Check it out!

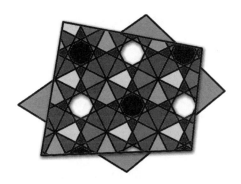

Rudyard Kipling Unveils the Mist from the East

Joseph Rudyard Kipling is a classic example of an author whose talents have been maligned by many of his peers but whose writings are beloved by his public. Kipling wrote largely about the East—about a complex land whose background, politics, and cultures the West could barely imagine.

Born in 1865 in Bombay, India, to educated, artistic English parents, Rudyard Kipling received his formal education in England, but not under the best circumstances. The neglect from foster parents hired to oversee his education damaged Kipling's eyes. Later in the United Services College, Kipling thrived with better care, more freedom, and, above all, more books to read. And he began to write.

Even as a boy, his writing gained notice. A newspaper in London printed his work. His parents had his verses printed and bound in India. Homesick perhaps, or maybe ambitious, Kipling returned to India, and by the time he was seventeen he had begun a career in journalism—if he wanted it.

He was absorbing India all over again. Now he would write about her in his *Barrack-Room Ballads*; in his short stories, such as *The Phantom 'Rickshaw*; and in his books for children, such as *Puck of Pook's Hill*, *The Jungle Book*, and our classic, *Kim*. Ever more successful, in 1907 Kipling became the first English writer to receive the Nobel Prize.

Although he married an American—the sister of his literary agent—lived in America, and traveled extensively, Kipling returned to England, where he died in 1936.

Kipling, the classic author, opened our hearts and our minds with his rich storytelling to a fascinating land that he knew and loved.

Presentation of Rudyard Kipling Script

Rudyard Kipling is the classic example of an author who writes of another time and another place with a wit, wisdom, and insight that transcend those boundaries of time and place.

The 1800s are not too removed for most readers, but the East, until fairly recently, has been cloaked in mystery for most of us in the West. Certainly most of us find it difficult to understand life under the rule of the Raj in 1800 India. Luckily we can turn to a writer like Rudyard Kipling, whose ballads, stories, and novels introduce us to the people and the culture from those times, from those lands that lie far to our east.

This script, using excerpts from Kipling's poetry and highlighting his novel *Kim*, is one step in the direction for a better understanding of this so-called inscrutable East. It is unique in that eighteen students can take part, including the Announcer. However, for a smaller cast of only ten readers, the lines for Storytellers 9 through 16 can be reassigned to Storytellers 1 through 8.

Hindi words are explained in the continuity of the script. All appear in a standard dictionary, except *chela*, which means disciple.

Stage Props

Reading stands for the cast, if possible (17 or 9)

Tall stools or chairs (17 or 9)

Hand Props

Scripts for each participant (18 or 10, plus one for the teacher)

Black folders for scripts

Rudyard Kipling Unveils the Mist from the East

Production note: Kim and Storytellers 1–8 as placed; Babu, 9; Pink Dominoes, 10, 11;
Files-on-Parade readers, 12, 13, 14; Curator, 15; Lama, 16

```
            X        X X
            9        10 11

XXXX                            X X X
5 6 7 8                         12 13 14

XXX                               X X
2 3 4                             15 16

        X                   X
        1                   Kim

              Announcer
```

Announcer:	*(Enters and takes center stage)* Welcome, friends, to Storyteller Theatre, where we present the classics you know—or maybe don't know, but classics that no one wants to miss. They're good; they're cool. And today's subjects are no exception—for today we celebrate the classic writing of Joseph Rudyard Kipling as he unveils life in earlier times in the mysterious country of India.
Storyteller 1:	There's only one Rudyard Kipling—poet, short story writer, novelist, Nobel Prize winner, and a patriot to be reckoned with.
Storyteller 4:	Patriot? Of what country? He sounds English.
Announcer:	Good guess—but it's more complicated than that. *He's* more complicated than that.
Storyteller 5:	Uh, oh. I can tell a muddle is coming up.
Announcer:	*Au contraire*, folks. Very simple. The man's an Englishman—but born in India. And now we're off on our journey to the mysterious land, the misty East, with the incomparable writer—Rudyard Kipling. *(Bows, exits)*
Storyteller 2:	I knew it—confusion right off the bat. The mysterious and misty East. What does that mean, anyway?
Storyteller 5:	Like—the place is hard to figure out—like it's exciting, different, unknown—a complete mystery, at least to us.
Storyteller 4:	Oh, I get it. We're talking India—Marco Polo—the Spice Trade—the Silk Road. Yeah! The Jewel in the Crown.
Storyteller 6:	The jewel. What jewel? And in what crown? Elucidate!
Storyteller 2:	Oh, that's great—*elucidate*. And we haven't even touched the Indian words.

Storyteller 7: Jewel in the Crown? Not a problem—dip back to 1865.

Storyteller 5: I've got that one—the Civil War ends. Grant and Lee. Appomattox.

Storyteller 8: Nice try. Think big—think India. Bombay. Kipling is born that year in that place. India's had a war, too—an Indian uprising—this one for Independence.

Storyteller 5: In the meanwhile, who's in charge? India's huge. Look at the map!

Storyteller 8: The country was under British rule—the Raj. In fact, when Kipling was twelve, Queen Victoria was crowned the Empress of India.

Storyteller 5: Got it! India belonged to the British Empire. India's the Jewel in the Crown!

Storyteller 7: And Kipling was all for it. After all, these were his roots.

Storyteller 1: Which brings us to his parents—both English, who, immediately after they married, moved to Bombay, India—where Kipling's father became the principal of an art school. Then Rudyard is born—and soon after, a daughter.

Storyteller 2: So, Rudyard Kipling grows up in India, writes stories, becomes famous, and lives happily ever after.

Storyteller 7: You know that's too good to be true. Imagine, instead, trauma, fear, pain, misery. The parents, thinking they were doing the right thing, sent the children to England to be educated. Rudyard was only six years old.

Storyteller 3: English tradition, but six? That's pretty young. What went wrong?

Storyteller 7: The Kiplings sent the children to a coastal town to stay with people they didn't even know. They had picked their names from a newspaper ad. Turns out these foster parents were horrible people. Rudyard nearly went blind from lack of care and physical abuse.

Storyteller 3: You know, he may have had a terrible time, but I think he used some of that experience in his stories—like in his novel about that little boy in India, Kim.

Storyteller 7: Right. And later in the book, when Kim attends boarding school, Kipling used experiences from *his* boarding school days.

Storyteller 4: I guess his mother finally yanked him away from those terrible people. But did he stay in England?

Storyteller 5: Yes. He enrolled in a school at Westward Ho!, another coastal town—like Bombay and Southsea. This was a good place this time. Now he could read anything and everything—and write.

Storyteller 6: He probably wrote for the school paper, right?

Storyteller 1: Yes, and he wrote a piece for a London paper—which paid him a whole guinea.

Storyteller 2: Uh huh. A guinea. *E-lucidate*—how much would that be?

Storyteller 1: In those days?—about five dollars and ten cents. Not much.

Storyteller 3: But just think—he's a schoolboy, and his work gets printed in a very important newspaper! I bet his parents were proud.

Storyteller 1: Proud? They'd already had some of his verses printed up and bound into a real book with a real name—*Schoolboy Lyrics*.

Storyteller 4: Sounds like he's doing okay in England. But wasn't he homesick?

Storyteller 8: He must have been. He left school and returned to India. Right away he went to work on a newspaper in Lahore, up north. By the time he was seventeen, he was the assistant editor.

Storyteller 2: You mean he switched from poetry to journalism?

Storyteller 7: Not exactly. He was writing and learning to write even better—to polish, organize, cut down. Journalism's good for all that.

Storyteller 2: But he can't just hang around a newspaper office and become famous for stories and books. Can he?

Storyteller 6: You know what? Kipling did! He kept his job, soaked up all the Indian culture he could and kept on writing and publishing. His stories and ditties became really popular in India—and in England.

Storyteller 2: Excuse me—ditties? What are ditties?

Storyteller 6: Simple stuff—little poems. Most of them told a story, with a soldier as the hero. Take the ditty "Pink Dominoes." Two young ladies at a costume ball wear masks to disguise their faces, and each is wearing a domino—a pink cloak. Listen:

Pink Dominoes **1:**
Jenny and me were engaged, you see,
On the eve of the Fancy Ball;
So a kiss or two was nothing to you
Or any one else at all.

Pink Dominoes **2:**
Jenny would go in a domino—
Pretty and pink but warm;
While I attended, clad in a splendid
Austrian uniform.

Pink Dominoes **1:**
Now we had arranged, through notes exchanged
Early that afternoon,
At Number Four to waltz no more,
But to sit in the dusk and spoon.

Pink Dominoes **2:**
When three was over, an eager lover,
I fled to the gloom outside;
And a Domino came out also
Whom I took for my future bride.

Pink Dominoes **1:**
That is to say, in a casual way,
I slipped my arm around her;
With a kiss or two (which is nothing to you),
And ready to kiss I found her.

Pink Dominoes **2:**
She turned her head and the name she said
Was certainly not my own;
But ere I could speak, with a smothered shriek
She fled and left me alone.

Pink Dominoes **1:**
Then Jenny came, and I saw with shame,
She'd doffed her domino;
And I had embraced a stranger's waist—
But I did not tell her so.

Storyteller 6: More verses—it's not the end, but you get the hang of it.

Storyteller 1: Listen to these lines from another ditty called "What Happened":

Babu: Hurree Chunder Mookerjee, pride of Bow Bazar,
Owner of a native press, 'Barrister-at-Lar,'
Waited in the Government with a claim to wear
Sabres by the bucketful, rifles by the pair.

Storyteller 3: The barrister's a lawyer, right? But swords and guns?

Storyteller 2: Sounds like the Old West—not the East. Say that name again.

Babu: Hurree Chunder Mookerjee.

Storyteller 7: Kipling liked that name, I think.

Storyteller 4: It has a rhythm all right. Huree Chunder Mookerjee. I like it!

Storyteller 6: You're not alone. The critics went wild. Kipling became *the* new writer of the day. Famous, and he's still young, in his early twenties. And now his book *The Man Who Would Be King* is out.

Storyteller 2: I saw that movie. It was on TV. I loved it! Talk about a different land. In that movie, India looked exciting, unusual, different.

Storyteller 1: Actually, his stories reveal more and more about India—like *The Jungle Book*. Remember Mowgli and Baloo, the bear?

Storyteller 6: And Bagheera, the black panther! I loved it—the law of the jungle!

Storyteller 7: Even when he goes back to England—to live in London—he turns out more tales and ballads set in India. Most of them had to do with army barracks life—like "Danny Cheever." Here's the opening:

Files-on-Parade: "What are the bugles blowin' for?" said Files-on-Parade.

Color-Sergeant: "To turn you out, to turn you out," the Colour-Sergeant said.

Files-on-Parade: "What makes you look so white, so white?" said Files-on-Parade.

Color-Sergeant: "I'm dreadin' what I've got to watch," the Colour-Sergeant said.

Storyteller 13: For they're hangin' Danny Deever, you
     can hear the Dead March play,
The regiment's in 'ollow square—they're
     hangin' him to-day;
They've taken of his buttons off an' cut his
     stripes away,
An' they're hangin' Danny Deever in the morning.

Files-on-Parade: "What's that so black agin the sun?" said Files-on-Parade.

Color-Sergeant: "It's Danny fightin' 'ard for life," the Color-Sergeant said.

Files-on-Parade: "What's that that whimpers over 'ead?" said Files-on-Parade.

Color-Sergeant: "It's Danny's soul that's passin' now," the Color-Sergeant said.

Storyteller 13: For they're done with Danny Deever,
     You can 'ear the quickstep play,
The regiment's in column, an' they're
     Marchin' us away;

Ho! the young recruits are shakin', an'
   they'll want their beer today,
After hangin' Danny Deever in the mornin'.

Storyteller 8: Whew! That reminds me of that poem "Gunga Din" about the Indian boy, who carries water for the soldiers. That was a movie, too. In the poem, the soldiers treat him like a slave, but when Gunga Din dies, saving a soldier, the man finally admits—

Babu: Though I've belted you an' flayed you.
By the livin' Gawd that made you,
You're a better man than I am, Gunga Din!

Storyteller 4: These stories or ditties or ballads are not very jolly.

Storyteller1: Life in India was not very jolly for everyone in the 1800s.

Storyteller 5: They had a caste system in those days. That's c-a-s-t-e. Cast with an e.

Storyteller 6: Right. Everybody placed in a category. At the top were the priests. Then came the warriors; then the farmers and other workers; at the very bottom were the Untouchables. They had nothing.

Storyteller 1: Kipling writes about them all, even when he's living in Vermont.

Storyteller 2: How did he get to Vermont?

Storyteller 6: Kipling married an American lady, and they lived in Vermont for about six years. Then they moved back to England for good. And the books just poured out of him until he died in 1936.

Storyteller 3: I guess he could write anywhere.

Storyteller 8: With his imagination, yes. He had soaked up India. He could invent animals and characters that walked, or crawled, right out of the different castes in India. Take Hurree Chunder Mookerjee.

Storyteller 2: That name again!

Storyteller 8: Matter of fact, that name pops up a lot in Kipling's novel, *Kim*.

Storyteller 4: Which takes place in Pakistan—which was also under British rule.

Storyteller 3: So Mookerjee is in the novel *Kim*. Who—or what—is Mookerjee?

Storyteller 8: Well, he's native Indian and a part *(Pause)* of the Great Game—the Great Game was the British Secret Service—and our boy, Kim, becomes part of that.

Storyteller 4: Even as a boy? What can he do?

Storyteller 8: Not a lot at first, but the Secret Service men recognize his talents and his background. Listen, as Kipling describes Kim in his novel:

Storyteller l: Kim was English. Though he was burned black as any native; though he spoke the vernacular by preference, and his mother-tongue in a clipped uncertain sing-song; though he consorted on terms of perfect equality with the small boys of the bazaar; Kim was white—a poor white of the very poorest.

Storyteller 7: His mother had married Kimball O'Hara, an Irishman serving in the British Army. But she died of cholera, and the half-caste woman who looked after him—who smoked opium and pretended to keep a second-hand furniture shop—told the missionaries that she was Kim's mother's sister. She claimed to be Kim's aunt.

Storyteller 1: His father, O'Hara, drifted away, till he came across the woman who took opium and learned the taste from her, and died as poor whites die in India.

Storyteller 4: And this little boy, Kim, grows up to become a spy? Pretty strange background for your James Bond type.

Storyteller 1: Wait. There's more. After O'Hara's death, the woman sewed his army papers—and Kim's birth certificate—into a leather amulet-case, which she strung around Kim's neck. Kim's father had told the woman the papers were magic—that on no account was Kim to part with them. Then he made a prophecy about Kim's future. But the woman mixed it up good when she told it to Kim later:

Storyteller 5: "And some day," she said confusedly remembering O'Hara's prophecies, "there will come for you a great red bull on a green field, and the colonel riding on his tall horse, yes, and . . . nine hundred devils."

Kim: Ah, I shall remember. A red bull and a colonel on a horse will come, but first, my father said, come the two men making ready the ground for these matters. That is how, my father said, they always did; and it is always so when men work magic.

Storyteller 1: Kim lived in a life as wild as that of the Arabian Nights, but missionaries and secretaries of charitable societies could not see the beauty of it. His nickname through all the wards was Little Friend of all the World.

Storyteller 5: The woman who looked after him insisted with tears that he should wear European clothes—trousers, a shirt, and a battered hat. Kim found it easier to slip into Hindu or Mohammedan garb . . . the costume of a low-caste street boy.

Storyteller 3: Well, I see one talent Kim has. He's already a master of disguise. He can pass for English, and he can pass for a native. I should think that trait would be useful for the Secret Service.

Storyteller 8: Oh, they recognize it. Plus, they see he is quick and clever. But Kim slows down when he meets a religious man from a monastery in Tibet, high in the Himalaya Mountains. Listen, as Kipling describes the lama coming toward Kim:

Storyteller 5: There shuffled round the corner, from the roaring Motee Bazar, such a man as Kim, who thought he knew all castes, had never seen. He was nearly six feet high, dressed in fold upon fold of dingy stuff like horse-blanketing, and not one fold of it could Kim refer to any known trade or profession.

Storyteller 8: At his belt hung a long open-work iron pencase and a wooden rosary such as holy men wear. On his head was a gigantic sort of tam-o'-shanter.

Storyteller 7: His face was yellow and wrinkled, like that of Fook Shing, the Chinese bootmaker in the bazaar. His eyes turned up at the corners and looked like little slits of onyx.

Storyteller 1: This holy man, this lama, has come looking for the Wonder House—the great city museum. Kim, who seems to know all things, takes the lama to the Sahib, the curator of the museum.

Storyteller 7: The office was but a little wooden cubicle partitioned off from the sculpture-lined gallery. Kim laid himself down, his ear against a crack in the heat-split cedar door, and, following his instincts, set himself to listen and watch.

Storyteller 8: Most of the talk was altogether above his head—until he hears the lama explain to the curator why he is on this journey as a pilgrim.

Lama:	I know nothing—nothing do I know—but I go to free myself from the Wheel of Things by a most broad and open road . . . for as a pilgrim to Holy Places I acquire merit.
Storyteller 2:	Merit? This is becoming mysterious. My teacher used to mark my best papers with a check-plus-good.
Storyteller 6:	Not that kind of merit. The lama wants to achieve virtue—for his future life. By visiting Holy Places, he earns spiritual credits.
Storyteller 2:	So he's on a religious journey?
Storyteller 6:	And a quest to find a special river—as he tells the curator:
Lama:	But there is more . . . a river . . . whose nature . . . is that whoso bathes in it washes away all taint and speckle of sin.
Curator:	So it is written.
Lama:	*(Sighs)* Where is that river, Fountain of Wisdom . . . the River of the Arrow?
Curator:	*(Sadly)* I do not know. I do not know.
Lama:	Surely thou must know!
Curator:	If I knew, think you I would not cry it aloud?
Lama:	We are both bound, thou and I, my brother. But I—I go to cut myself free. Come also!
Curator:	Alas, I am bound.
Storyteller 5:	After a while, the lama strode out, head high in the air, and pausing an instant before the great statue of a Bodhisat in meditation, brushed through the turnstiles.
Storyteller 6:	Kim followed like a shadow. What he had overheard excited him wildly. This man was entirely new to all his experience, and he meant to investigate further.
Kim:	And what didst thou worship within?
Lama:	I worshipped none, child. I bowed before the *Excellent Law*.
Storyteller 4:	Kim accepted this new god, the Excellent Law, without emotion. He already knew a few score.
Kim:	And what dost thou do?
Lama:	I beg. I remember now it is long since I have eaten or drunk. What is the custom of charity in this town? In silence, as we do of Tibet, or speaking aloud?
Kim:	Those who beg in silence starve in silence. Give me the bowl. I know the people of this city—all who are charitable. Give, and I will bring it back filled.
Storyteller 1:	So Kim becomes the disciple, the *chela* of the old man. Together they are going to search for the lama's River of the Arrow and for Kim's Red Bull on a green field. It was Kismet, as Kim would say—Fate—that had brought them together.
Storyteller 4:	In harmony now, they set off to find lodging at the Kashmir Serai.
Kim:	I have a friend there. Come!
Storyteller 5:	The hot and crowded bazaars blazed with light as they made their way through the press of all the races in Upper India, and the lama mooned through it like a man in a dream. . . . Half pushed, half towed, he arrived at the high gate of the

Kashmir Serai: that huge open square over against the railway station, surrounded with arched cloisters where the camel and horse caravans put up on their return from Central Asia.

Storyteller 7: Kim, fending the lama between excited men and excited beasts, sidled along the cloisters to the far end, nearest the railway station where Mahbub Ali, the horse-trader, lived when he came in from that mysterious land beyond the Passes of the North.

Storyteller 6: Kim had had many dealings with Mahbub in his little life, especially between his tenth and his thirteenth year, and the big burly Afghan, his beard dyed scarlet with lime (for he was elderly and did not wish his gray hairs to show), knew the boy's value as a gossip. *(Slowly)* Sometimes he would tell Kim to watch a man who had nothing whatever to do with horses: to follow him for one whole day and report every soul with whom he talked.

Storyteller 4: Kim would deliver himself of his tale at evening, and Mahbub would listen without a word or gesture. It was intrigue of some kind, Kim knew, but its worth lay in saying nothing whatever to anyone except Mahbub, who gave him beautiful meals all hot from the cookshop at the head of the Serai, and once as much as eight annas in money.

Storyteller 5: Now, hitting a bad-tempered camel on the nose, he halted before a dark arch and slipped behind the bewildered lama.

Kim: "He is here. *(Calling)* Ohé, Mahbub Ali!"

Storyteller 6: The horse-trader, his deep, embroidered Bokhariot belt unloosed, was lying on a pair of silk carpet saddle-bags, pulling lazily at an immense silver hookah. He turned his head very slightly at the cry, and seeing only the tall, silent lama, chuckled in his deep chest.

Storyteller 2: *(Pause)* So what does he say? Does he help them? Look—is this Mahbub Ali really just a horse trader?

Storyteller 3: I bet it's a cover for what he really does. I bet he's part of the Great Game—you know, all that spying he tells Kim to do. It was just practice for the real thing.

Storyteller 1: You think so, huh? Can't give it all away—but must say that the horse-trader, Mahbub Ali turns up later on—and later still.

Storyteller 2: Okay. Question: If the Great Game is the British Secret Service, aren't Englishmen in charge? Or—who is in charge?

Storyteller 1: Ah, yes, you want to meet the Colonel Sahib—who buys horses from our horse-trader. Maybe you want to learn about the man who deals in pearls—the jeweler, Lurgan Sahib.

Storyteller 2: Do I? Maybe. One thing is strange—they're all called Sahib.

Storyteller 3: You're really slow. Sahib means sir or master. If you're from a low caste and want to speak to your superiors, you use Sahib. See?

Storyteller 2: Oh, thank you so much—Sahib! Have we met all the players?

Storyteller 1: Not quite. While the jeweler, Lurgan Sahib, is training him, Kim's told to sit and wait for a half hour. At the end of that time enters a hulking obese Babu whose stockinged legs shook with fat.

Storyteller 2: Not a pretty picture. Okay—what's a Babu?

Storyteller 3: Another name for mister—for an Indian gentleman. This Babu has a price on his head and is known by his letter and number: R.17.

Storyteller 2: Oooh—like double-o-7.

Storyteller 7: Got it! Well, Kim meets him *again*, four days later on a train: His companion was the whale-like Babu, who, with a fringed shawl wrapped round his head, and his fat open-worked stockinged left leg tucked under him, shivered and grunted in the morning chill.

Storyteller 8: And again they meet at the house of a maharanee who has been buying medicines from a traveling hakim. Kim doesn't trust the drugs or the hakim who peddles them.

Kim: "Who is the hakim, Maharanee?"

Storyteller 5: The maharanee tells him the hakim is "A wanderer, as thou art, but a most sober Bengali from Dacca—a master of medicine."

Storyteller 4: Kim *has* to meet the hakim. When he does, Kim bristles like an expectant terrier. To outface and down-talk a Calcutta-taught Bengali, a voluble Dacca drug-vendor, would be a good game.

Storyteller 5: The two have a war of words—then when they are alone, the hakim speaks, hardly more than shaping the words with his lips:

Babu: "How do you do, Mr. O'Hara? I am jolly glad to see you again."

Storyteller 6: Kim's hand clenched. . . . Anywhere on the open road, perhaps, he would not have been astonished; but here in this quiet backwater of life, he was not prepared for Hurree Babu.

Storyteller 2: Huree? Wait. Wait! That's—Hurree Chunder Mookerjee.

Announcer: *(Enters to center)* Well done! You've discovered him *again*—Mookerjee, another master of disguise. But of course, you haven't met all the members of the Great Game, have you? For example, E.23. No? Or the District Superintendent of Police—who plays the Game—just in time? No?

Storyteller 3: Hold on. What about the lama and his search for The River of the Arrow? And the Red Bull on the green field in Kim's prophecy?

Announcer: *(Shrugs)* You know what? It's all in that novel, *Kim*—all about the mysterious East waiting to be discovered by you. Read the book—see Rudyard Kipling lift the veil from that mist of the East. Read it. You'll see! *(Announcer bows. Cast bows)*

Edgar Allan Poe Weaves a Dark World

The man casts a long shadow—Edgar Allan Poe, poet, philosopher of aesthetics, and one of the most dramatic storytellers of all time. The man is a classic, and his work has been honored at home and abroad for nearly two hundred years.

Yet Edgar Allan Poe was born and lived under another shadow—one of poverty and neglect. Orphaned at age two when his father disappeared and his mother died, Poe was taken in by foster parents. He never knew financial security. He never had the love of complete acceptance until he moved into his aunt's house with her and his young cousin, his grandmother, and his brother. This little ménage, though ill-fated, for a while provided Poe the stability he had longed for and needed.

His parents, traveling American actors, left him no visible legacy, but somehow they had willed him a sense of the dramatic that inspired him and eventually gave us unforgettable stories and ideas.

Born in 1809, Poe gradually emerged into a literary time that sparkled with the likes of Byron, Dickens, Stevenson, Thoreau, Longfellow, Hawthorne, and the Brontes. Like them, Poe was different—bold and unusual. His poem "The Raven" made him a celebrity. His psychological twists, innovative detective stories, his rhythms, and his critiques of poetry, drama, song-writing, and even furniture further impressed the world.

In 1836, Poe married his thirteen-year-old cousin, Virginia—but lost her a decade later to the ravages of that same tuberculosis that had claimed his mother and his brother. When Virginia died, Poe seemed to go off the deep end. Alcohol became a terrible problem. He became physically and emotionally ill. In 1849 he collapsed on the streets of Baltimore. Then, after lying comatose for days in a hospital, Poe died at age forty.

Presentation of Edgar Allan Poe Script

Chills and thrills—the macabre and the beautiful thread their way through the poems and stories of Edgar Allan Poe. Intrinsically dramatic, the stories do not call for any histrionics from the young readers. The words speak for themselves!

In this script, excerpts from some of Poe's most famous writings are interspersed with background information on Poe himself. Lines of his poetry are represented by "The Raven," "Al Aaraaf," and "Annabel Lee."

In addition, scenes are dramatized from *M.S. Found in a Bottle* (read by Storytellers 5, 6, and 7), *The Cask of Amontillado* (Storytellers 8 and 9), *The Facts in the Case of Monsieur Valdemar* (Storytellers 10, 11, and 12), and *The Tell-Tale Heart* (Storytellers 13 and 14). A brief visit to "The Raven" (Storytellers 15, 16, 17, and 18) and a reading in unison of "The Bells" draw the show to a close.

Eighteen Storytellers, plus the Announcer, compose the cast. Poe's narrators and characters are inevitably male. However, when casting, the Announcer and Storytellers 1, 2, 3, 4, 11 and 15, 16, 17, and 18 are appropriate choices for girl readers.

Stage Props

18 reading stands, if possible

18 tall stools or chairs

Hand Props

19 scripts (plus one for the teacher)

19 black folders for scripts

Edgar Allan Poe Weaves a Dark World

```
              X  X  X
              10 11 12

              X  X  X  X
              15 16 17 18

  X   X                          X   X
  13  14                         8   9

X   X   X   X                  X   X   X
1   2   3   4                  5   6   7
```

Announcer

—◆◇◆—

Announcer: *(Enters to center stage)* Welcome to Storyteller Theatre—where classic surprises pop up with classic books and classic authors. Here, little-known facts will creep into your knowledge of great literature. You will amaze your family. Delight your friends. Broaden your love for books. And with a subject like Edgar Allan Poe, scare yourself to death. *(Pause)* Interested? Good. Then let's enter the weird world of sound and sense and sensations created by that master of terror and tintinnabulation—Edgar Allan Poe.

Storyteller 2: *(Shudders but smiles)* Oh, I'm scared! Already I'm thinking "It was a dark and stormy night—"

Storyteller 4: You have it all wrong. It goes, "Once upon a midnight dreary, while I pondered, weak and weary, over a quaint and curious—"

Announcer: *(Interrupting)* "The Raven." Sensational! I think you have it, friends. I think we're ready—for this mystery tour with Mister Poe.

Storyteller 1: Please. Mystery mister? Enough of that!

Announcer: Ah, but language is all, friends—witness the sounds, sense, and sensations as we enter the dark world of Edgar Allan Poe! *(Exits)*

Storyteller 3: Whew! We'd better backtrack—start at the beginning.

Storyteller 2: Okay, but let's not begin with his words. I'd say start with his life. Try Boston— 1809—when Poe was born to poor traveling actors.

Storyteller 1: Good choice. Edgar Allan Poe, the child of struggling actors.

Storyteller 3: Actors? There you see—Poe was destined to be dramatic!

Storyteller 2: Maybe. Certainly born to struggle, and in more ways than one. Before Poe is even two years old, his father disappears, and his mother dies in Richmond, Virginia. Not a very good beginning.

Storyteller 4: Not for Poe or his brother or their baby sister. Poe's grandparents take in his brother, William Henry. Another family takes the baby, and the tobacco merchant John Allan and his wife take in Poe.

Storyteller 3: Allan was a merchant? That sounds like money—not poverty.

Storyteller 1: You'd think so. But money has to come your way; you face poverty if it doesn't. Poe learned that early on. He was an orphan, and he remained an orphan. John Allan never adopted him.

Storyteller 4: But he gave him his name—Edgar Allan. Very strange. Poe was an extraordinary student, too—but we admit he did have a bad record.

Storyteller 3: Bad record? Are you suggesting girls?

Storyteller 2: No—but it might have been true. Certainly when he was young, Sarah Elmira Royster caught his eye. But no trouble with the girls. He often was dismissed from school—like the University of Virginia—for gambling or for debts. He was even dismissed from West Point, but only because Mr. Allan refused to pay his fees.

Storyteller 3: Of course, right in character for Mr. Allan—a real tightwad.

Storyteller 2: He was. But Poe really wanted to be in the Army—and become an officer, at that—even though that seems a stretch to being a writer.

Storyteller 4: It might, but he was good at the military. Before he entered West Point, he'd already been in the Army, under a different name. And what's more, he'd already published—by himself—his first book of poems—under a different name. Seems Poe could be a soldier *and* a writer.

Storyteller 3: And he's how old—eighteen? Well, I confess I'm impressed.

Storyteller 2: But apparently John Allan was not. The so-called father and his son seem to have had serious problems—not very simpatico.

Storyteller 1: Right, and misfortune struck again. Mrs. Allan died. First, Poe lost his real mother. Now his foster mother was gone. He and Mr. Allan did reconcile after that, but then Poe moved to Baltimore where a real publisher printed his second volume of poetry.

Storyteller 4: And that first poem, "Al Aaraaf," is something else! Listen:
All Nature speaks, and ev'n ideal things
Flap shadowy sounds from visionary wings—
But ah! not so when, thus, in realms on high
The eternal voice of God is passing by,
And the red winds are withering in the sky!

Storyteller 3: Now there's a sound of words—*(Carefully)*—red winds withering!

Storyteller 1: There's more to come in a third volume of his poetry—like one of my favorites, "To Helen." Poe writes of Helen's beauty—her classic face—and he calls her Psyche, after a beautiful Greek princess.

Storyteller 3: You're describing Helen—as in Helen of Troy?

Storyteller 1: *(Nods)* As in. But the big question is—who was the real Helen of that poem? Or, for that matter, who was Annabel Lee? Remember how that poem goes?

Storyteller 4: I do. Listen:
It was many and many a year ago,
   In a kingdom by the sea
That a maiden there lived whom you may know
   By the name of Annabel Lee;
And this maiden she lived with no other thought
   Than to love and be loved by me.

Storyteller 3: Well, we don't know which young lady Poe was writing about.

Storyteller 1: No, but we do know he finally had a taste of real family life. He moved into his aunt's house—joining her and his cousin, Virginia, his grandmother, and his brother, who had become seriously ill with tuberculosis. But Poe had contentment for a while, until—

Storyteller 2: Tragedy came once more—his brother died. But then, good fortune: Poe won fifty dollars in a short story contest.

Storyteller 3: I know. That was *M.S. Found in a Bottle*. It was about a manuscript placed in a bottle and tossed into the ocean. Talk about a sensational story—it's this one!

Storyteller 2: You can tell it's sensational right off from that quote in French. It goes something like this: a person who has only a moment to live no longer has anything to hide.

Storyteller 1: It's the story of a sea voyage gone bad. The writer of the manuscript and an old Swedish sailor are the only survivors of a horrible storm. For five days the storm has been sweeping their ship toward the South Pole—certain death. Listen to the narrators:

Storyteller 5: We waited in vain for the arrival of the sixth day—that day to me has not yet arrived—to the Swede, never did arrive.

Storyteller 6: Every moment threatened to be our last—every mountainous billow hurried to overwhelm us.

Storyteller 5: I could not help feeling the utter hopelessness of hope itself, and prepared myself gloomily for that death which I thought nothing could defer beyond an hour, as, with every knot of way the ship made, the swelling of the black stupendous seas became more dismally appalling.

Storyteller 7: At times we gasped for breath . . . at times became dizzy with the velocity of our descent into some watery hell.

Storyteller 6: We were at the bottom of one of these abysses, when a quick scream from my companion broke fearfully upon the night.

Storyteller 7: "See! see!" cried he, shrieking in my ears, "Almighty God! See! see!"

Storyteller 5: As he spoke, I became aware of a dull sullen glare of red light which streamed down the sides of the vast chasm where we lay, and threw a fitful brilliancy upon our deck.

Storyteller 6: Casting my eyes upwards, I beheld a spectacle which froze the current of my blood. At a terrific height directly above us, and upon the very verge of the precipitous descent, hovered *(Pause)* a gigantic ship of, perhaps, four thousand tons.

Storyteller 7: Staggering as far aft as I could, I awaited fearlessly the ruin that was to overwhelm. Our own vessel was at length ceasing from her struggles, and sinking with her head to the sea.

Storyteller 5: The shock of the descending mass struck her . . . and the inevitable result was to hurl me, with irresistible violence, upon the rigging of the stranger. As I fell the ship hove . . . and went about; and to the confusion ensuing, I attributed my escape from the notice of the crew.

Storyteller 6: They paid me no manner of attention . . . and seemed utterly unconscious of my presence . . . [They] glide to and fro like the ghosts of buried centuries.

Storyteller 7: As I imagined, the ship proves to be in a current . . . a tide which, howling and shrieking by the white ice, thunders on. . . . Oh, horror upon horror! the ice opens suddenly to the right, and to the left, and we are whirling dizzily, in immense concentric circles, round and round.

Storyteller 5: The circles rapidly grow small—we are plunging madly within the grasp of the whirlpool—

Storyteller 6: And amid a roaring, and bellowing, and thundering of ocean and of tempest, the ship is quivering—oh, no!

Storyteller 7: And—going down!

Storyteller 3: *(Pause)* Whew! A shipwreck, a ghost ship, disaster! No wonder this story won the contest. Poe must have been famous after that.

Storyteller 1: You'd think so. But he still wasn't making any real money—so now he turned to journalism.

Storyteller 3: He began to write for newspapers?

Storyteller 4: And magazines. He wrote, edited, and published stories, articles, pamphlets. Then he began reviewing. He became a literary critic. And Poe made a really good critic. He was tough, but he was good. Brilliant. Good sense. *(Slight pause)* But then he made a very strange move.

Storyteller 1: Yes, he married his thirteen-year-old cousin, Virginia. Then they moved to New York, but he was not earning any money there. So, they moved to Philadelphia for more magazine jobs. Then New York published his first novel, and Philadelphia published his first book of short stories—*Tales of the Grotesque and Arabesque*.

Storyteller 2: Grotesque? Something fantastic or bizarre. But ar-a-besque? I haven't a clue what that means.

Storyteller 4: Okay. Arabesque is a really difficult ballet position, but for writing it has to mean some complicated plot—strange patterns, you know.

Storyteller 1: How about *The Cask of Amontillado* for an arabesque plot?

Storyteller 4: That will do—*The Cask of Amontillado* is grotesque, as well!

Storyteller 3: Okay, now let's unravel the plot. Take the title first. Cask: a barrel. Amontillado is a Spanish sherry—or wine.

Storyteller 1: Good. *The Cask of Amontillado*. Now, place: Italy, and the time is carnival time, like Mardi Gras. The characters? One man and his so-called friend. Listen to the beginning and be ready to shudder:

Storyteller 8: The thousand injuries of Fortunato I had borne as I best could;

Storyteller 9: But when he ventured upon insult, I vowed revenge.

Storyteller 3: Excuse me—what had Fortunato done, or said?

Storyteller 4: Ssh. The narrator doesn't tell us—yet. But he has a plan.

Storyteller 3: Does he ever! First, he is *very* friendly with Fortunato.

Storyteller 8: I continued, as was my wont, to smile in his face, and he did not perceive that my smile *now* was at the thought of his immolation.

Storyteller 1: Immolation—look it up, or guess. Kill will do. Sacrifice. Destroy.

Storyteller 7: Right you are. So, as *friends*, they meet.

Storyteller 8: It was about dusk, one evening during the supreme madness of the carnival season, that I encountered my friend. He accosted me with excessive warmth, for he had been drinking much.

Storyteller 9: The man wore motley . . . and his head was surmounted by the conical cap and bells. I was so pleased to see him, that I should never have done wringing his hand.

Storyteller 1: So Fortunato is dressed like a clown—or jester, and the narrator tricks him into visiting his wine vaults to taste his Amontillado. He flatters Fortunato over and over until the man actually insists on entering the vaults. So they go deeper and deeper underground.

Storyteller 9: We passed through a range of low arches, descended, passed on, and descending again, arrived at a deep crypt, in which the foulness of the air caused our flambeaux rather to glow than flame.

Storyteller 8: At the most remote end of the crypt there appeared another less spacious. Its walls had been lined with human remains, piled to the vault overhead, in the fashion of the great catacombs of Paris. . . . "Proceed," I said; "herein is the Amontillado."

Storyteller 9: He stepped unsteadily forward, while I followed immediately at his heels. In an instant he had reached the extremity of the niche . . . and stood stupidly bewildered.

Storyteller 8: A moment more and I had fettered him to the granite. In its surface were two iron staples, distant from each other about two feet, horizontally. From one of these depended a short chain, from the other a padlock. Throwing the links about his waist, it was but the work of a few seconds to secure it. He was too much astounded to resist. Withdrawing the key I stepped back from the recess.

Storyteller 9: "The Amontillado!" my friend cried, not yet recovered from his astonishment.

Storyteller 8: "True," I replied, "the Amontillado." As I said these words I busied myself among the pile of bones of which I have before spoken. Throwing them aside, I soon uncovered a quantity of building stone and mortar . . . and with the aid of my trowel, I began vigorously *(Slowly)* to wall up the entrance of the niche.

Storyteller 9: There was a low moaning cry from the depth of the recess . . . a long and obstinate silence . . . furious vibrations of the chain . . . a succession of loud and shrill screams.

Storyteller 8: I forced the last stone into its position; *(Slowly)* I plastered it up.

Storyteller 2: *(Pause)* No more Fortunato? He's walled up? Is that the end?

Storyteller 9: Read the end, friend. You might hear the jingling of the bells.

Storyteller 3: That's a gruesome death! Grotesque!

Storyteller 1: True—but apparently Poe had death and wine and drunkenness on his mind. Life was not going well for him. His young wife had suffered a hemorrhage, and he had taken to drink.

Storyteller 2: Hemorrhage? Sounds like tuberculosis again—first his mother, then his brother, now Virginia. And his jobs—he seems to be batting around from pillar to post.

Storyteller 4: He even went to Washington, D.C., to see about a job under President Tyler. But he blew that possibility—too much drink.

Storyteller 1: He had one good thing happen, though. He won another literary prize—this time a hundred dollars for his story *The Gold Bug*. He'd already invented a master detective. That was a first. He actually started us on that twisty tail of detective stories.

Storyteller 3: How come his stories are so spooky—kind of out of this world?

Storyteller 2: You mean like his tales about mesmerism?

Storyteller 3: I don't know—what's mes-mer-ism? *(Pause)* Wait a minute. Doesn't that have something to do with hypnosis?

Storyteller 1: Yes, but back then they called it falling under the *magnetic influence*. Whatever you call it, it means one person putting another person to sleep—or something like sleep. Scientists were experimenting with mesmerism, wondering if dying could be stopped—or if science could start life up again.

Storyteller 2: Wow. You're talking about *Frankenstein* now.

Storyteller 4: Old stuff to Poe, but that book sure sparked his imagination! Take Poe's story *The Facts in the Case of Monsieur Valdemar*, where a man on the brink of death asks to be—mesmerized.

Storyteller 3: Hypnotised while he's dying? Why would he want that?

Storyteller 1: The narrators explain it this way—listen:

Storyteller 10: My attention, for the last three years, had been repeatedly drawn to the subject of Mesmerism; and about nine months ago, it occurred to me, quite suddenly, that . . . no person had as yet been mesmerized *in articulo mortis*.

Storyteller 2: Got it! *Articulo mortis*—almost dead. Well, at any rate, dying.

Storyteller 10: It remained to be seen, first, whether, in such condition, there existed in the patient any susceptibility to the magnetic influence;

Storyteller 11: Secondly, whether, if any existed, it was impaired or increased by the condition;

Storyteller 10: Thirdly, to what extent, or for how long a period, the encroachments of Death might be arrested by the process. In looking around me for some subject by whose means I might test these particulars, I was brought to think of my friend, Monsieur Ernest Valdemar.

Storyteller 11: For some months previous to my becoming acquainted with him, his physicians had declared him in a confirmed phthisis. *(thy-sis)*

Storyteller 3: Uh, oh. The man was dying?

Storyteller 1: He was. He had reached phthisis—the last stages of tuberculosis.

Storyteller 2: Tuberculosis again. That disease haunts Poe! So what happens? He mesmerizes Valdemar—and then what?

Storyteller 4: Valdemar does not die—at first.

Storyteller 3: At first? I told you—spooky!

Storyteller 1: You haven't heard the half of it! Listen. He goes on:

Storyteller 10: I now feel that I have reached a point of this narrative at which every reader will be startled into positive disbelief. It is my business, however, simply to proceed.

Storyteller 11: There was no longer the faintest sign of vitality in Monsieur Valdemar; and concluding him to be dead, we were consigning him to the charge of the nurses, when Monsieur Valdemar *spoke*—I had asked . . . if he still slept. He now said:

Storyteller 12: "Yes—no—I *have been* sleeping—and now—now *I am dead*."

Storyteller 11: It was evident that, so far, death (or what is usually termed death) had been arrested by the mesmeric process. . . . To awaken Monsieur Valdemar would be merely to insure his instant, or at least his speedy, dissolution.

Storyteller 3: Dissolution? Would he dissolve—or disappear?

Storyteller 4: Ssh. Listen!

Storyteller 10: Mesmerized after *nearly seven months* . . . we finally resolved to make the experiment of awakening, or attempting to awaken him.

Storyteller 11: "Monsieur Valdemar, can you explain to us what are your feelings or wishes now?"

Storyteller 12: There was an instant return of the hectic circles on the cheeks: the tongue quivered, or rather rolled violently in the mouth. . . . and at length the same hideous voice broke forth: "For God's sake—quick—quick—put me to sleep—or, quick—waken me—quick—*I say to you that I am dead!*"

Storyteller 10: I . . . earnestly struggled to awaken him. . . . I am sure that all in the room were prepared to see the patient awaken. For what really occurred, however, it is quite impossible that any human being could have been prepared. As I rapidly made the mesmeric passes, amid horrible cries of "Dead! Dead!"

Storyteller 11: Absolutely *bursting* from the tongue and not from the lips of the sufferer, his whole frame at once—within the space of a single minute, or less, shrunk—

Storyteller 10: Crumbled—absolutely *rotted* away beneath my hands. Upon the bed, before that whole company, there lay a nearly liquid mass of loathsome—of detestable putrescence.

Storyteller 3: Dissolution? Oh, no! Dissolution? That's melting away!

Storyteller 1: Of course this story was all made up—but when it was published, the public thought the mesmerizing experiment had really happened. They believed it. But then, people have always been curious about the moment of death. Poe was curious—and afraid.

Storyteller 4: He truly feared death. He particularly feared being buried alive.

Storyteller 1: Nervous yet? Sick to your stomach? Spooked? Scared? Good. I think you're in the right mood for another grotesque tale. *(Slowly) The Tell-Tale Heart.* Listen to the narrators in this story:

Storyteller 13: Why *will* you say that I am mad? The disease had sharpened my senses—not destroyed—not dulled them. Above all was the sense of hearing acute. I heard all things in the heaven and in the earth. I heard many things in hell.

Storyteller 14: How, then, am I mad? I can tell you the whole story. *(Pause)* It is impossible to say how first the idea entered my brain; but once conceived, it haunted me day and night. Object there was none. Passion there was none.

Storyteller 13: I loved the old man. He had never wronged me. He had never given me insult. For his gold I had no desire.

Storyteller 14: I think it was his eye! Yes, it was this! One of his eyes resembled that of a vulture—a pale blue eye, with a film over it. Whenever it fell upon me, my blood ran cold; and so by degrees—very gradually—I made up my mind to take the life of the old man, and thus rid myself of the eye forever.

Storyteller 13: Every night, just at twelve, I looked in upon him while he slept. And . . . there came to my ears a low, dull, quick sound, such as a watch makes when enveloped in cotton. I knew *that* sound . . . the beating of the old man's heart. . . . The beating grew louder, louder! I thought the heart must burst. . . . The old man's hour had come! . . . With a loud yell . . . I leaped into the room.

Storyteller 14: *(Pause)* He shrieked only once—once only. . . . For many minutes the heart beat on with a muffled sound. . . . At length it ceased.

Storyteller 13: I worked hastily, but in silence. First of all I dismembered the corpse. I cut off the head and the arms and the legs. I then took up three planks from the flooring of the chamber, and deposited all.

Storyteller 14: It was four o'clock—still dark as midnight. As the bell sounded the hour *(Pause)*, there came a knocking at the street door.

Storyteller 3: *(Pause)* Well, who was it? What about the heart? Come on, tell!

Storyteller 4: Oh—perhaps another time. Or—check the library.

Storyteller 2: We get it—to be continued. See the next installment. Whatever.

Storyteller 1: This is heady stuff. Poe was churning out one tale after the other, and selling them to magazines, then publishing them in books.

Storyteller 4: Along with those reams of criticism and the poems. Oh, don't forget the poems!

Storyteller 2: He must have been making money now.

Storyteller 1: Some money; some fame—but tragedy at home. Virginia again. It was that terrible tuberculosis. She was really ill by 1847. She died that year.

Storyteller 2: But Poe? He must have been devastated.

Storyteller 1: He virtually fell apart. He became ill himself. He drank too much. Rumors said he'd gone mad. But he was still working—writing, lecturing, planning. He tried to connect with other women—even with his first love, Sarah Elmira, a widow now.

Storyteller 3: Oh, I can feel it—the gradual running down. Yet he's not too old.

Storyteller 2: How much more time?

Storyteller 1: Two years. He collapsed on the streets of Baltimore. They took him to the hospital. He lay in a coma for four days and finally died October 7, 1849. He was only forty.

Storyteller 4:   When I think of Poe, I see him in his study, reading, writing, or thinking—haunted by that enormous black bird, the raven:

Storyteller 15:   Once upon a midnight dreary, while I pondered, weak and weary,
Over many a quaint and curious volume of forgotten lore—

Storyteller 16:   While I nodded, nearly napping, suddenly there came a tapping,
As if some one gently rapping, rapping at my chamber door.

Storyteller 17:   "Tis some visitor," I muttered, "tapping at my chamber door—
Only this and nothing more."

Storyteller 18:   Open here I flung the shutter, when, with many a flirt and flutter
In there stepped a stately Raven of the saintly days of yore.

Storyteller 15:   Not the least obeisance made he; not a minute stopped or stayed he;
But, with mien of lord or lady, perched above my chamber door—

Storyteller 16:   Perched upon a bust of Pallas just above my chamber door—
Perched, and sat, and nothing more.

Storyteller 17:   Then this ebony bird beguiling my sad fancy into smiling,
By the grave and stern decorum of the countenance it wore,

Storyteller 18:   "Though thy crest be shorn and shaven, thou," I said, "art sure no craven,
Ghastly grim and ancient Raven wandering from the Nightly shore—

Storyteller 15:   Tell me what thy lordly name is on the Night's Plutonian shore!"
Quoth the Raven, "Nevermore."

Storyteller 16:   And the Raven, never flitting, still is sitting, *still* is sitting
On the pallid bust of Pallas just above my chamber door;

Storyteller 17:   And his eyes have all the seeming of a demon's that is dreaming,
And the lamp-light o'er him streaming throws his shadow on the floor;

Storyteller 18:   And my soul from out that shadow that lies floating on the floor
Shall be lifted—nevermore!

Announcer: *(Enters to the side)* Oh, the rhythm of that man—the sounds—the sense and the thrill of his sensations—how they ring in your ears!

Storyteller 1:   Like his poem, "The Bells"? Listen:
Keeping time, time, time
In a sort of Runic rhyme,
To the tintinnabulation that so musically wells

Storytellers All: From the bells, bells, bells, bells,
Bells, bells, bells—

Announcer: From the jingling and the tinkling of the bells. *(Enters to center stage)* Ring on, Poe! Read on, friends—for thrills and terrors by a master of them all, that classic author—Edgar Allan Poe!

William Shakespeare and His Phantasmagoria of Fantasies

"Not of an age but for all time," said playwright Ben Jonson of his illustrious peer, William Shakespeare. And so say we. From his first recorded production in 1592, scholars and theatre lovers have continued to honor Shakespeare as the supreme genius of English drama.

Although Shakespeare continues to inspire and illuminate us, his work can intimidate the young. And why not? Many references are beyond their ken. The language is four hundred years old. But think of the people and the plots in those plays—the delicious comedies—the heartbreaking tragedies. These, the youthful readers can grasp.

In *The Tempest* Prospero concludes, "our little life is rounded by a sleep." Shakespeare's own life began in Stratford-upon-Avon, April 23, 1564. That life was gently "rounded" in that same English village on April 23, 1616. But what amazing accomplishments came from those fifty-two years!

Born into a merchant's family, Shakespeare received a good, solid education in Stratford, but his ambitions and talents led him to pursue a life in the theatre in London. He married Anne Hathaway and had three children with her, but his lifelong occupation as an actor, playwright, and producer kept him in London.

He forsook neither his family nor his roots, but instead he invested in Stratford and eventually retired there—after writing nearly forty plays by himself and collaborating on others. He wrote long narrative poems and scores of beautiful sonnets. Through these works he speaks to us still, enriching our minds and touching our hearts.

Presentation of William Shakespeare Script

William Shakespeare and his plays—what a challenge to youthful readers and playgoers. If, however, these young people can look beyond their expectations and explore the fantasy in Shakespeare's plays, they may come to understand and enjoy the ideas and music of Shakespeare.

This script introduces salient facts about Shakespeare and examines some of his fantastic elements in *A Midsummer Night's Dream*, *Twelfth Night*, *The Tempest*, *Macbeth*, and *Hamlet*. Storytellers and audience will see how spirits, witches, ghosts, transformations, magic, and fortune-telling heighten Shakespeare's plays.

The script calls for twenty-one readers plus the Announcer. Suggestions for positions on stage appear on the first page of the script. Storytellers will take their places and sit. Indications to stand appear throughout the script for those who read the character parts (e.g., Oberon, Titania, etc.).

At the conclusion, Storytellers will "talk Shakespeare," with a short barrage of famous quotations from the incredible scope of Shakespeare's dramatic literature and poetry.

Stage Props

5 reading stands, if possible

5 tall stools or chairs (for Storytellers 1, 2, 3, and 4, and Shakespeare)

16 chairs for other readers

Hand Props

22 scripts (plus l for the teacher)

22 black folders for scripts

William Shakespeare and His Phantasmagoria of Fantasies

Production note: Places in addition to Storytellers 1, 2, 3, 4 and Shakespeare—Oberon, 5; Titania, 6; Anne, 7; Duke, 8; Prospero, 9; Ariel, 10; Caliban, 11; the three Witches, 12, 13, 14; Banquo, 15; Macbeth, 16; Marcellus, 17; Horatio, 18; Bernardo, 19; Hamlet, 20

```
              X X X X X
             10 11 17 18 19


        X X X X X X X X X X
        5  6  7  8  9 12 13 14 15 16

    X X X X              X        X
    1 2 3 4         Shakespeare  20

              Announcer
```

—◀◈▶—

Announcer:	Welcome, my friends, to Storyteller Theatre, where the classics and their authors come alive! Shakespeare is our man today—that classic storyteller from England, William Shakespeare—the bard of Stratford, the genius of the boards! *(Indicates Shakespeare)*
Storyteller 4:	Hold on—what's this *bard* thing? Barred from what?
Announcer:	I believe we're talking a bit of culture here—old-timey knowledge. A bard, my friend, is a singing poet—if you don't know it.
Storyteller 3:	Uh, oh. I'd say we're in for a rough time this time.
Storyteller 2:	*(Simpleton)* I like to sing, but I don't think poetry is my cup of tea.
Announcer:	Just you wait, my friend. We're gonna knock your socks off with the most exciting poetic fantasies that ever hit the boards!
Storyteller 4:	Hold on—the boards?
Announcer:	Theatre, my friend. The stage—the boards, and the greatest genius who wrote for the boards was and is William Shakespeare.
Storyteller 2:	*(Innocently)* Oh, another old author. *(Sing-song the dates)* Born April twenty-third, fifteen sixty-four. Died April twenty-third, sixteen-sixteen, age fifty-two. *(Pause)* Thank you very much. I think I'll go back to that poetry.
Announcer:	You do that, friend. However, you just might run into Shakespeare, after all—his plays or his sonnets. In any case, we're pushing on.
Storyteller 2:	Good. Don't worry about me. I'll try to follow your lead.
Announcer:	Excellent. So—on to our genius of the theatre, William Shakespeare, and to his poetic, dramatic travels into the strange and unknown—where things are not always what they seem. Straight ahead to Shakespeare's Phantasmagoria of Fantasies! *(Announcer bows, waves to audience, and leaves the stage)*

Storyteller 1:	Our apologies, Mr. Shakespeare, and to your lady, Mistress Anne.
Shakespeare:	*(Stands)* Not at all. *(Nods at Anne)* We understand. You had a lively bit of dialogue there. Hmm. Perhaps I could use some of that fantasy in another play.
Storyteller 3:	Another play? I count nearly forty already, plus those you wrote with others. Comedies and tragedies, yes. But fantasies?
Shakespeare:	Not complete fantasies, perhaps, but I did incorporate a little magic and a few characters that can't really exist. *(Pause)* At least, I don't think they can. *(Smiles)* Who knows for sure?
Storyteller 3:	Like those fairies in *A Midsummer Night's Dream*?
Storyteller 1:	Like Peaseblossom, Cobweb, Moth, and Mustardseed.
Storyteller 2:	*(Giggles)* What names! They must come from a fantasy!
Storyteller 3:	They do. And don't forget that tricky spirit in *A Midsummer Night's Dream*—Puck. He's one of my favorites—always interfering with real people and always messing up things.
Storyteller 1:	Ah, yes, Puck and the magic purple flower. One drop of that magic potion and you fall in love with the very next person—or thing.
Storyteller 2:	*(Giggles)* Really? Where do we get this magic flower?
Shakespeare:	Well, the love thing in the play is all Puck's doing, but you see, he serves Oberon, king of the fairies. And when Oberon quarrels with his queen, Titania, he decides to teach her a lesson with the magic flower. Listen to Oberon's plan:
Oberon:	*(Stands)* Fetch me that flower; the herb I show'd thee once: The juice of it on sleeping eyelids laid, will make either man or woman madly dote upon the next live creature that it sees. Fetch me this herb: and be thou here ere the leviathan can swim a league.
Storyteller 4:	Hold it right there. Leviathan? League?
Storyteller 3:	I have this one. Leviathan—sea monster. League—three or four miles. So Oberon tells Puck to be fast—to bring him the flower in less time than it takes a sea monster to swim three or four miles.
Storyteller 4:	I got it. And Puck's answer?
Storyteller 1:	He says, "I'll put a girdle round about the earth in forty minutes."
Storyteller 4:	I don't think I'll ask about *girdle*. I think it means to encircle the earth. But then what does Oberon say he'll do with the flower?
Oberon:	Having once this juice, I'll watch Titania when she is asleep, and drop the liquor of it in her eyes: The next thing when she waking looks upon—be it on lion, bear, or bull, on meddling monkey, or on busy ape—she shall pursue it with the soul of love. And ere I take this charm off from her sight—as I can take it with another herb, I'll make her render up her page to me. *(Pause)* Who comes here? I am invisible, and I will overhear their conference. *(Sits)*
Storyteller 4:	Invisible is always good. So does the flower work?
Shakespeare:	Better than I'd hoped, but Puck does make a few mistakes. The wrong people fall in love, but he thinks fast and remedies that.

Storyteller 2:	What about Oberon's plan to trick his queen?
Shakespeare:	Oh, that plan is a great success.
Storyteller 1:	Here goes: In the forest, Puck finds a group of honest workmen rehearsing their play for a celebration. One of them is taking a nap.
Storyteller 3:	Uh, oh. The sleeping eyelids thing.
Storyteller 1:	Exactly. Puck gives one sleeping man, Bottom, an ass's head. Then the purple flower works its charms on the sleeping Titania.
Storyteller 3:	Ooh, this is getting good!
Storyteller 1:	Indeed. Bottom wakes up singing, and Titania, hearing him sing (or bray), wakes up!
Titania:	*(Stands)* I pray thee, gentle mortal, sing again: Mine ear is much enamour'd of thy note. So is mine eye enthralled to thy shape; and thy fair virtue's force perforce doth move me, on the first view, to say, to swear, I love thee. *(Sits)*
Storyteller 2:	And Titania falls in love—with a donkey?
Storyteller 3:	*(Giggles)* Oh, that's amazing! And we believe it!
Shakespeare:	It's a fantasy, of course, my young friend. A fantasy where people are changed, literally transformed, by spirits and love.
Storyteller 1:	Transformation also happens in *Twelfth Night*. In the very beginning of that comedy, the Duke of Illyria says—
Storyteller 4:	Hold on. Where's Illyria? Did I miss that land in geography class?
Shakespeare:	You might have, of course. It's a fanciful place. Oh, it really existed at one time, but I've never seen it. Actually, I didn't travel at all—except occasionally to my home in Stratford—to see my wife and three children.
Storyteller 3:	Oh, interesting! You were married—but you lived in London?
Shakespeare:	Yes, to both questions. I was married, and I did live in London.
Storyteller 3:	But why? Wasn't it hard to commute to Stratford?
Shakespeare:	Yes, but I couldn't be a merchant like my father. True, I did have a good education. I could read Latin—some Greek. But what could I do? Then, one day, a group of traveling actors came to Stratford, and I knew that's what I wanted to do—become an actor.
Storyteller 2:	You couldn't do that in Stratford?
Shakespeare:	*(Laughs)* Indeed not! Stratford was a very small town. To train as an actor I had to find the best theatres. I had to go to London.
Anne Hathaway:	*(Stands)* And leave me with the baby.
Shakespeare:	*(Smiles)* My wife, Anne Hathaway. We married when I was about eighteen. Anne was a bit older—twenty-six. We had a daughter shortly thereafter, Susanna.
Anne Hathaway:	And in 1585, less than two years later, we had twins—Judith and Hamnet. But three children or not, William went to London!
Shakespeare:	To earn a living for us all. I had to leave.
Anne Hathaway:	What could I say—or do? I stayed with the children in Stratford.

Shakespeare:	And I, in London, learned to act. And I began to write plays.
Anne Hathaway:	But it's your poetry I love, Will. Your sonnets fill my heart. *(Sits)*
Storyteller 3:	Oh, good! See, I knew we'd end up talking about poetry.
Storyteller 1:	Actually, we're doing two things at once. Shakespeare wrote many of his plays in poetic form.
Shakespeare:	Well, of course, I didn't invent that. Others wrote in poetry, too.
Storyteller 1:	But you did it so well! As the Duke says in *Twelfth Night*—
Storyteller 2:	In the mythical land of Illyria—
Duke:	*(Stands)* If music be the food of love, play on. Give me excess of it; that surfeiting, the appetite may sicken and so die.
Storyteller 3:	That's just beautiful! *(Pause)* What does it mean?
Storyteller 1:	He's lovesick. He fancies he's madly in love with a rich Countess, Olivia, who doesn't love him. So, if music feeds love, maybe if he hears enough music, he'll get sick of his infatuation. Listen to him:
Duke:	So full of shapes is fancy, that it alone is high-fantastical. *(Sits)*
Storyteller 1:	High-fantasical shapes! But in *Twelfth Night*, people cause these transformations, not spirits or flowers—people.
Storyteller 4:	Here's the story of *Twelfth Night*: A young woman, Viola, is washed ashore from a shipwreck. She puts on men's clothing and becomes Cesario, a page for the Duke, who sends her with love notes to the Countess Olivia. But Olivia doesn't love the Duke. She falls in love with Cesario, the messenger—Viola, of course.
Storyteller 3:	Stop, already! That is very confusing.
Shakespeare:	*(Laughs)* Actually, it's meant to be confusing.
Storyteller 4:	*(Pretty fast)* Then Viola's twin brother shows up. He falls in love with Olivia, and she falls in love with him, only she thinks *he* is *her*—Viola—who by now is in love with the Duke.
Storyteller 3:	*(Big breath)* That's too much! And all this because of a shipwreck?
Shakespeare:	Yes! *(Laughs)* We had a lot shipwrecks in the sixteenth century. All that exploring, you know, commanded by Her Majesty, Queen Elizabeth. She sent Sir Francis Drake around the world and up the Orinoco. Englishmen started the first colony in Newfoundland.
Storyteller 4:	And later, Puritans from England landed on Plymouth Rock.
Shakespeare:	That's in America, correct? After my time, I'm afraid—but no doubt another English adventure. Some were highly successful. Others not, often because of terrible storms that wrecked the ships.
Storyteller 1:	Storms? Ah. That's the last play you wrote alone, *The Tempest*.
Shakespeare:	It is. *(Smiles) The Tempest*—perhaps my favorite play of them all.
Storyteller 1:	*The Tempest* actually opens with a tempest—thunder and lightning, and a ship that seems to be sinking.
Storyteller 3:	Hold on—*seems* to be sinking?

Storyteller 1:	One man has whipped up this storm to gain revenge.
Storyteller 3:	Okay. That's fantastic—one man can't whip up a storm.
Storyteller 1:	Prospero can—he and his magic spirit, Ariel.
Storyteller 3:	Oh, well. Magic. We're into fantasy again. Okay. Who's Prospero?
Storyteller 1:	He was the Duke of Milan—until his greedy brother took over his position as the Duke. But instead of killing Prospero outright, this greedy brother set Prospero and his daughter adrift in the sea. A dreadful event. Prospero remembers it well.
Prospero:	*(Stands)* They hurried us aboard a bark; bore us some leagues to sea; where they prepar'd a rotten carcass of a boat, not rigg'd, nor tackle, sail, nor mast; the very rats instinctively had quit it: there they hoist us, to cry to the sea that roar'd to us; to sigh to the winds, whose pity, sighing back again did us loving wrong.
Storyteller 3:	That's terrible! What happened to them?
Storyteller 1:	They landed on an uninhabited island.
Storyteller 2:	Bad scene! How does Prospero get even with his horrid brother?
Shakespeare:	Through the tempest. Twelve years later—still on the island—Prospero discovers his brother is on a nearby ship, so he decides to create a storm. He calls upon his servant, the magic spirit, Ariel.
Storyteller 3:	Ariel—a magic spirit? Where did he come from?
Shakespeare:	Ah, Ariel served the witch, Sycorax. Ariel was her prisoner.
Storyteller 3:	I see. Fantasy land again—how come he's Prospero's servant now?
Storyteller 1:	Ariel *owes* him. Prospero saved him from the witch's spell. But now Ariel demands his freedom. Prospero objects to that and reminds Ariel of his duty. He speaks harshly to Ariel:
Prospero:	Dost thou forget from what a torment I did free thee?
Ariel:	*(Stands)* No.
Prospero:	Thou liest, malignant thing! Has thou forgot the foul witch, Sycorax? . . . Hast thou forgot her?
Ariel:	No, sir.
Prospero:	Thou knowest she was banished. . . . Is not this true?
Ariel:	Ay, sir.
Prospero:	This blear-eyed hag was hither brought with child, and here was left by sailors.
Storyteller 3:	A hag who is a witch was going to have a baby? Was this Ariel?
Storyteller 1:	No. Ariel was the *servant* of Sycorax. Prospero explains all:
Prospero:	Thou wast a spirit too delicate to act her earthy and abhorr'd commands. Refusing her grand 'hests, she did confine thee . . . into a cloven pine.
Storyteller 2:	Ariel refused to obey the witch, so she stuck him in a tree? Whew!
Prospero:	Imprison'd, thou dids't painfully remain a dozen years; within which space she died, and left thee there. . . . Then was this island (save for the son that she did litter here, a freckled whelp, hag-born) not honour'd with a human shape.
Ariel:	Yes: Caliban her son.

Prospero:	Dull thing, I say so; he, that Caliban whom now I keep in service. Thou best know'st what torment I did find thee in. . . . It was mine art, when I arriv'd, and heard thee, that . . . let thee out. *(Ariel sits)*
Storyteller 3:	I get it. Prospero releases Ariel from the witch's spell.
Storyteller 1:	And, in return, Ariel must serve Prospero. So, when the survivors of the sinking ship reach the island, Ariel becomes invisible. Then with "noises, sounds and sweet airs" he lures the men to Prospero.
Storyteller 3:	I think I feel sorry for little Caliban.
Storyteller 6:	You needn't. He is not a cute little baby. He's grown—hideous—a witch's child. Listen as he calls up his mother's evil curse:
Caliban:	*(Stands)* As wicked dew as e'er my mother brush'd with raven's feather from unwholesome fen, drop on you both! A south-west blow on ye, and blister you all o'er. . . . All the charms of Sycorax, toads, beetles, bats, light on you! *(Sits)*
Prospero:	Abhorred slave. . . . Hag-seed, hence! *(Sits)*
Storyteller 4:	This is too real. It's like a myth gone bad.
Storyteller 1:	But what is real? What is fantasy—imagined? Near the end of the play, Prospero's speech pulls it all together. Mr. Shakespeare?
Shakespeare:	*(As Prospero)* Our revels now are ended: these our actors, as I foretold you, were all spirits, and are melted into air, into thin air.
Storyteller 3:	The people and the spirits disappear. Was this a dream?
Shakespeare:	Perhaps. If it was, it was a fantastical dream.
Storyteller 2:	I keep wondering why you mixed spirits in with real people.
Shakespeare:	Well, I confess. Mixing spirits and people is not original with me.
Storyteller 2:	I know we do it all the time in the movies. Only those spirits are more like aliens from another world. We have a lot of trouble trying to control them.
Storyteller 3:	Like in *Godzilla*—or how about *The Lord of the Rings*?
Shakespeare:	Have you read *The Odyssey*? *The Iliad*? I found plenty of struggles there between the humans and their gods.
Storyteller 4:	But in those stories, usually the gods are in control. They win out.
Shakespeare:	Ah, but in *The Tempest*, the humans are in control.
Storyteller 3:	Well, I think it's very dramatic! I'd love to play one of the spirits.
Shakespeare:	As an actor myself, I know it is fun—rewarding. So when I started to write plays—and act in them—I tried to make them dramatic.
Storyteller 2:	I get it—spooky parts, fierce parts, like Bottom says in *A Midsummer Night's Dream*—"a part to tear a cat in."
Storyteller 3:	Oh, lions and tigers, eh? That's very fierce.
Shakespeare:	Good! Our audiences wanted to be scared, amazed—surprised.
Storyteller 4:	That couldn't have been very difficult for the theatre in your time. You didn't have any competition—no television, no movies, no videos—not even radio. Did people have to pay to see your plays?

Shakespeare:	*(Laughs)* True—we had little competition. And yes, people paid. The rich paid two or three cents to sit on benches to see our shows.
Storyteller 2:	And the poor people—standing room for them?
Shakespeare:	*(Laughs again)* They paid one cent for standing and walking-around room. Oh, it was noisy. As actors we had plenty of competition. You have no idea what went on in our theatres!
Storyteller 3:	Oooh, what went on? Tell!
Shakespeare:	Oh, nothing too bad. We had Orange Girls who strolled around during the play selling oranges. Boys sold tobacco, apples, nuts—and peddled the latest news. *(Pause)* But it's the dogs I remember.
Storyteller 3:	Oh, that's sweet! I wish I had a pet. I love dogs.
Shakespeare:	That's all very well, indeed. Unfortunately, the dogs that came to the theatre were not trained to use—shall I say, "the facilities"?
Storyteller 4:	You mean—they made a mess—right there in the theatre?
Shakespeare:	In our day, we had no facilities for dogs or people.
Storytellers 2, 3, 4:	Euuuuuw!
Storyteller 1:	But you had a new theatre.
Shakespeare:	We did. I was part of a company of actors—the King's Men. We commissioned the Globe Theatre—built it in London just before the turn of the century—in 1599. I might add I not only acted and wrote for the King's Men, I shared in their profits as well.
Storyteller 2:	Hold on! The King's Men—and Women?
Storyteller 4:	I know the answer to that. All the acting parts were played by men.
Storyteller 2:	No actresses? What about the Queen, Titania?
Storyteller 4:	Played by a man.
Storyteller 2:	Viola, who becomes Cesario?
Storyteller 4:	Played by a man, who then plays the man, Cesario, in disguise.
Storyteller 3:	I love it! *(Pause)* But what about Romeo and Juliet?
Storyteller 4:	Men—both parts played by men.
Storyteller 3:	Fantastic! Men played The Weird Sisters in *Macbeth*? Well, the audience pays attention to them. They're spooky, fierce, and scary.
Storyteller 1:	They're spirits from another world who can predict the future. They know what was, what is, and what will be. We start with thunder and lightning. *(Witches 1, 2, 3 stand)*
Shakespeare:	*(Smiles)* A good way to open the show, I thought. Listen:
Witch 1:	When shall we three meet again—In thunder, lightning or in rain?
Witch 2:	When the hurlyburly's done. When the battle's lost and won.
Witch 3:	That will be ere the set of sun.
Witch 1:	Where the place?

Witch 2:	Upon the heath.
Witch 3:	There to meet with Macbeth.
Witches 1, 2, 3:	Fair is foul, and foul is fair; Hover through the fog and filthy air.
Storyteller 1:	And then they vanish—only to meet, before the sun sets, with the two generals, Macbeth, the Lord of Glamis, and Banquo.
Witch 1:	All hail, Macbeth! hail to thee, Thane of Glamis!
Witch 2:	All hail, Macbeth! hail to thee, Thane of Cawdor!
Witch 3:	All hail, Macbeth, thou shalt be king hereafter!
Storyteller 4:	What *was*: Macbeth *was* of Glamis. What *is*? The *present* Thane of Cawdor has died. Macbeth is already the new thane. But what *will be*? Macbeth will become king.
Storyteller 1:	A riddle—but perfectly clear. But how does Macbeth become king? The witches don't say, but he kills the king to become king!
Storyteller 2:	And what's predicted for Banquo? Does he ask The Weird Sisters?
Banquo:	*(Stands)* To me you speak not. If you can look into the seeds of time and say which grain will grow, and which will not, speak then to me, who neither beg nor fear your hate.
Witch 1:	Lesser than Macbeth, and greater. *(Sits)*
Witch 2:	Not so happy, yet much happier. *(Sits)*
Witch 3:	Thou shalt get kings, though thou be none: So all hail, Macbeth and Banquo! *(Sits)*
Storyteller 1:	Another riddle, this time about Banquo—who "shalt get kings." Macbeth sees that will threaten his line, his dynasty. Plus, does Banquo suspect he killed the king? What should Macbeth do now?
Storyteller 3:	He kills Banquo, too? I don't think I'm going to like this next part.
Shakespeare:	Fair enough. It was a dastardly deed done by dastardly men.
Storyteller 3:	I guess that's the end of Banquo?
Storyteller 1:	Not exactly. Banquo next appears as a Ghost, invisible to all except Macbeth—and Macbeth is terrified by what he sees. Listen:
Macbeth:	*(Stands)* See there! Behold! Look! Lo! How say you? . . . Avaunt! and quit my sight! Let the earth hide thee! Thy bones are marrowless, thy blood is cold; Thou hast no speculation in those eyes which thou dost glare with! . . . Hence, horrible shadow! *(Sits)*
Storyteller 1:	Later, the witches return. They're making their hideous brew.
Witch 1:	*(Witches stand)* Round about the caldron go; in the poison'd entrails throw.
Witches 1, 2, 3:	Double, double toil and trouble: fire, burn; and, caldron, bubble.
Witch 2:	Fillet of a fenny snake, in the caldron boil and bake; eye of newt, and toe of frog, wool of bat, and tongue of dog, adder's fork and blindworm's sting, lizard's leg, and howlet's wing—for a charm of powerful trouble, like a hell-broth boil and bubble.
Witches 1, 2, 3:	Double, double toil and trouble. Fire, burn and caldron bubble. *(Witches 1, 2 sit)*

Witch 3:	Cool it with a baboon's blood. Then the charm is firm and good. *(Witch 3 sits)*
Storyteller 3:	Enough already! We see it all—murders in high places.
Storyteller 2:	Sounds like another murder in another play—*Hamlet*.
Storyteller 3:	Oh, that's my favorite play—*Hamlet, Prince of Denmark*.
Storyteller 1:	Well, you are bloodthirsty.
Storyteller 4:	But in this play, Hamlet's father is already dead. And it's his Ghost that reveals who murdered him. Right away, the Ghost appears.
Storyteller 3:	I know. That opening scene is spooky.
Shakespeare:	Good. I've always enjoyed playing the Ghost—even though I did write the part.
Storyteller 4:	A scene to tear a cat in! Midnight outside a castle. Soldiers are keeping watch. They've brought Hamlet's friend, Horatio, to see the Ghost, to see what they have seen—twice. Marcellus speaks:
Marcellus:	*(Marcellus and Bernardo stand)* Horatio says 'tis but our fantasy, and will not let belief take hold of him touching this dreaded sight, twice seen of us: Therefore, I have entreated him along with us to watch the minutes of this night; that, if again this apparition come he may approve our eyes and speak to it.
Horatio:	*(Stands)* Tush, tush, 'twill not appear.
Marcellus:	Peace, break thee off; look where it comes again!
Shakespeare:	Enter Ghost, armed.
Bernardo:	In the same figure, like the king that's dead.
Marcellus:	Thou art a scholar. Speak to it, Horatio.
Bernardo:	Looks it not like the king? Mark it, Horatio.
Horatio:	Most like—it harrows me with fear and wonder.
Bernardo:	It would be spoke to.
Marcellus:	Question it, Horatio. . . . It is offended.
Bernardo:	See it stalks away!
Horatio:	Stay! Speak, speak! I charge thee, speak!
Marcellus:	'Tis gone, and will not answer.
Shakespeare:	Is it the dead king? A ghost could be anything—take the shape of any person, any animal.
Storyteller 1:	It appears three more times. It still won't speak—until Horatio brings Hamlet to the watchtower and points to the Ghost.
Horatio:	Look, my lord, it comes! *(Marcellus, Bernardo, Horatio sit)*
Hamlet:	*(Stands)* Angels and ministers of grace defend us! Be thou a spirit of health or goblin damn'd, bring with thee airs from heaven or blasts from hell, be thy intents wicked or charitable, Thou com'st in such a questionable shape that I will speak to thee: I'll call thee Hamlet, King, father, royal Dane: O, answer me!
Storyteller 1:	It doesn't answer of course—not in front of the other soldiers. But the Ghost beckons Hamlet to follow him. Hamlet pleads with him:

Hamlet:	Where wilt thou lead me? Speak; I'll go no farther.
Storyteller 1:	Mr. Shakespeare—your part: The Ghost answers Hamlet.
Shakespeare:	I am thy father's spirit; doom'd for a certain term to walk the night, and, for the day, confin'd to waste in fires till the foul crimes done in my days of nature are burnt and purg'd away. . . . List, list, O, list! If thou didst ever thy dear father love.
Hamlet:	O God!
Shakespeare:	Revenge his foul and most unnatural murder.
Hamlet:	Murder!
Shakespeare:	Murder most foul, as in the best it is; but *this* most foul, strange, and unnatural. *(Hamlet sits)*
Storyteller 2:	*(Pause)* So what happened? Who murdered the king? How? Why?
Shakespeare:	*(Deep breath. Smiles)* Perhaps you might attend a performance of my play? Or you could buy a copy of it. In my day, that was not possible. But all is available to you, my friends—the mystery of King Hamlet's death and his revenge by Prince Hamlet, his son.
Storyteller 1:	*(Bows)* Thank you, Mr. Shakespeare—actor, playwright, poet! Our cup is nearly full. But before we bid our friends adieu, hark to these lines for your memory— to fill your heart as well.
Storyteller 2:	Some men are born great, some achieve greatness, and some have greatness thrust upon them. *Twelfth Night*
Storyteller 3:	Shall I compare thee to a summer's day? "Sonnet XVIII"
Storyteller 4:	Though this be madness, yet there is method in it. *Hamlet*
Storyteller 1:	To be, or not to be: that is the question. *Hamlet*
Storyteller 2:	Sweets to the sweet: farewell. *Hamlet*
Storyteller 3:	Something is rotten in the state of Denmark. *Hamlet*
Storyteller 4:	For mine own part, it was Greek to me. *Julius Caesar*
Storyteller 1:	O! this learning, what a thing it is. *Taming of the Shrew*
All stand and read:	Good night! Parting is such sweet sorrow! *Romeo and Juliet*
Announcer:	*(Enters and takes center stage)* They're talking Shakespeare! Fantastic! But a brief word to the wise from Prince Hamlet: "Speak the speech, I pray you, as I pronounced it to you, trippingly on the tongue." Ready? Dip into them! Shakespeare's Phantasmagoria of Fantasies! *(Smiles)* Farewell!

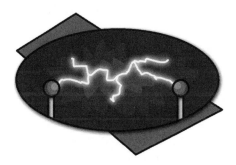

Mary Shelley Creates a Novel of Horror with *Frankenstein*

Nearly two hundred years ago, Mary Wollstonecraft Godwin Shelley, a bold and brilliant young woman, created, on a dare, one of the most intriguing horror tales of all literature—*Frankenstein*.

Born in 1797 London in the aftermath of Revolutionary times, Mary Shelley inherited all the fantasies and ideas that burgeoned with the new century and the Romantic Period that soon emerged.

Daughter of the pioneering feminist, Mary Wollstonecraft, and the erudite William Godwin, Mary Shelley was destined to exceed them both. Although her mother died shortly after Mary's birth, Mary learned to read voraciously and to write with skill and art under her father's careful tutelage.

In 1814, this petite, passionate, and intelligent young girl fell in love with the charismatic poet Percy Bysshe Shelley. Instantly drawn to each other, the two lovers ignored a probable scandal and eloped to Switzerland, marrying after the death of Shelley's wife.

While they were vacationing near their friend and fellow poet, Lord Byron, Mary accepted his challenge to write a ghost story. Still a teenager, but inspired by the grandeur of the Alps, she created a modern Prometheus—Victor Frankenstein—who creates the monster that still lives and thrills us in *Frankenstein*.

Mary and Percy Bysshe Shelley had three children, only one of whom survived. Shelley died in 1822, leaving Mary to carry on his legacy. She continued to write fiction, biographies, and travel articles until her death in 1851. But it is her crowning achievement of *Frankenstein*, first published in 1817, that became a classic for all time.

Presentation of Mary Shelley Script

The creative genius of Mary Wollstonecraft Godwin Shelley was fostered by the vibrant heritage of her crusading mother and the rich literary environment that her father provided—one that nourished her early, formative years.

Making a reality leap into the lives of classic authors often requires a generous lift from the historical facts and emotional circumstances that influenced those lives. Mary Shelley, the classic author of *Frankenstein*, takes on a more complete characterization if we connect her with her time, her place, and the people who influenced her and encouraged her talent—in particular, her parents and husband, Percy Bysshe Shelley.

This script, which investigates and celebrates Mary Shelley and *Frankenstein*, calls for ten Readers, including the Announcer. Except for the part of Mary, Storyteller parts may be read by either boys or girls. Storytellers 2, 3, and 4 in particular have light lines that question and respond. Storytellers 5, 6, 7, and 8, grouped together, share reading the excerpt from *Frankenstein*.

Stage Props

9 reading stands, if possible

9 tall stools or chairs

Hand Props

10 scripts (plus 1 for the teacher)

10 black folders for scripts

One copy of *Frankenstein* for Announcer to show at end of performance

Mary Shelley Creates a Novel of Horror with *Frankenstein*

```
        X X              X X
        5 6              7 8

                 X
               Mary

    X                       X X X
    1                       2 3 4


              Announcer
```

—◄◆►—

Announcer:	*(Steps to center stage)* Welcome to Storyteller Theatre—where we celebrate a born storyteller. Today, a storyteller who created a monster that will not die. You know this monster. He's been on television, in the movies, on the stage, and in comic books. But we are interested in his beginnings—with Mary Wollstonecraft Godwin Shelley, who created the monster from her imagination.
Storyteller 2:	How did she do that?
Announcer:	Ah—you mean what fueled her imagination?
Storyteller 3:	Well, something set her off—that monster, I mean.
Storyteller 2:	She sure has a monster name—Wollstonecraft.
Storyteller 1:	*(Loud whisper)* Ssh. She's English. That was her mother's name.
Announcer:	Hey, are you ready for this?
Storyteller 1:	We're ready.
Storyteller 4:	Yeah! Blood and guts! Monsters! Lead on!
Announcer:	*(Shakes head)* You know, I think you're going to be surprised. But let's begin. Let's explore the passionate Mary Wollstonecraft Shelley and her *Frankenstein*. *(Announcer exits)*
Storyteller 5:	Hey, this is getting interesting. So where are we?
Storyteller 1:	Jump back more than two hundred years—1797 to be exact—when Mary Wollstonecraft Godwin Shelley was born.
Storyteller 3:	With a name like that, she has to be good!
Storyteller 1:	Ha. Ha. Very funny. Her name was famous before she was born. First because of her mother—the first Mary Wollstonecraft.
Storyteller 3:	Well, I never heard of her.
Storyteller 1:	Too bad. She's one of the reasons we have girls in our class.
Storyteller 8:	Of course—Mary Wollstonecraft. She created waves back then with her so-called wild ideas. She thought girls should be taught the same things as boys.

Storyteller 3:	Sure, why not?
Storyteller 7:	It just wasn't done. Boys got the brainy education—not the girls.
Storyteller 6:	Now here's the shocker—she said that boys and girls should be taught together—and in the same classroom!
Storyteller 5:	Hey, that's a very good idea.
Storyteller 1:	Yes, but not a popular idea two hundred years ago. But she kept writing about it—and she became famous.
Storyteller 4:	Okay, we've got the Wollstonecraft thing down. Does the Godwin name belong to her father?
Storyteller 1:	Brilliant guess. Her father was William Godwin—another famous writer with radical ideas—and he was a philosopher.
Storyteller 3:	Two famous parents. One lucky baby.
Storyteller 1:	Not exactly. Mary's mother died only two weeks after little Mary was born.
Storyteller 4:	*(Sadly)* Ohh—
Storyteller 3:	Brothers or sisters?
Storyteller 5:	One half-sister, two years old. Fanny. So now her father had two little girls and no wife. *(Slight pause)* What could he do? He married again.
Storyteller 3:	Oh, that was good, wasn't it?
Storyteller 5:	Could be—but not in this case. His new wife also had two children. And the new Mrs. Godwin turned out to be the spittin' image of Cinderella's stepmother.
Storyteller 4:	Oh, that was bad?
Storyteller 8:	Wait—there's more. The stepmother had another baby, William.
Storyteller 3:	Blended family—Mr. and Mrs. Godwin and now five children.
Storyteller 7:	Yes, but Mary was the shining one for Mr. Godwin.
Storyteller 2:	Apple of her father's eye?
Storyteller 1:	He taught her everything, including how to write.
Mary:	Oh, yes! As a child I scribbled, and my favorite pastime . . . was to write stories. . . . Still, I had a dearer pleasure than this, which was the formation of castles in the air—the indulging in waking dreams . . . at once more fantastic and agreeable than my writings.
Storyteller 6:	But the books she read! Her father taught her to read two and three books at one time. He let her read anything she wanted.
Storyteller 2:	Like what, for instance?
Storyteller 6:	All kinds of books from his library—like history and science. She read about experiments—like Ben Franklin's with the kite, Galvani's and Volta's with—
Storyteller 4:	Electricity. Volta—voltage. Galvani—galvanism. I get it.
Storyteller 1:	She loved reading about those scientific experiments. But of course she read fiction, as well. Aesop's fables, Shakespeare—
Storyteller 3:	Oh. *Romeo and Juliet*, I suppose.
Storyteller 4:	"Romeo! Romeo, wherefore art thou?"

Storyteller 1:	Ha! Think *Hamlet*. Mary liked the part where the Ghost of King Hamlet appears from the mist and speaks: *(Spooky)* "List! List!" But beside these books, Mary also read her mother's novels—and she loved William Blake's strange illustrations—like the one of a huge man with burning eyes and clenched fists who stares down at two children in their bed.
Storyteller 5:	She even read *The Castle of Otranto*. Real Gothic—full of ghosts and giants—walls that fall down and statues that come to life.
Storyteller 3:	*(Whispers)* I heard about that. Statues that bleed through the nose!
Storyteller 2:	I guess these books didn't scare her.
Storyteller 5:	Not this little girl—she visited her mother's grave in the churchyard every day. You see, she was not happy with her stepmother. She missed her real mother—even though she never knew her. So, for comfort, she sat beside her mother's grave—among the burial vaults. There, in the graveyard, Mary could imagine her mother—who she probably thought would have loved and understood her, especially her daydreams.
Storyteller 6:	Not like the stepmother who wanted Mary to learn how to cook and clean house—not daydream or read all day.
Storyteller 1:	Or to listen to Mr. Godwin and his friends argue about religion, discuss science, or read aloud some of the new poetry—like that of Wordsworth or Samuel Coleridge.
Storyteller 3:	Coleridge? Maybe she heard *The Rime of the Ancient Mariner*.
Storyteller 7:	Actually, she did. One night, when her stepmother wasn't looking, Mary crept into the parlor and hid behind the furniture. That very night Coleridge read his poem.
Storyteller 4:	Oh, good for her! That's a poem about ships and sailors.
Storyteller 8:	But it's not a happy tale about ships and sailors. The ship is becalmed, and the sailors are dying of thirst. They're surrounded by water—but it's an ocean of—salt water. Coleridge writes—
Storyteller 7:	Water, water, every where, And all the boards did shrink; Water, water, every where, Nor any drop to drink.
Storyteller 3:	I remember. The ancient mariner bites his own arm and sucks the blood—just to get something to drink.
Storyteller 1:	Then he kills a seabird, an albatross. But the sailors believe this means more bad luck. So to punish the ancient mariner, the angry sailors hang the albatross about the mariner's neck. Fantastic ideas and stories like these flew to Mary's head and stayed there. Like that fantastic Greek myth she read about Prometheus.
Storyteller 2:	Oh, yes, really ancient god, Prometheus. Full of imagination. He sprinkled a handful of clay with water and made a man from it.
Storyteller 4:	A little clay statue? What's so great about that?
Storyteller 2:	That clay became more than a statue, thanks to the goddess, Athena. She breathed life into it. Animated it.

Storyteller 3:	The clay figure came alive? How'd she do that?
Storyteller 2:	Athena? It's a myth from the Greeks—from their imagination.
Storyteller 1:	Made up or not, I don't think Mary ever forgot that story.
Storyteller 8:	Or those books on science—or those experiments with electricity. In one experiment they shocked the leg of a dead frog—and the power of the electricity made it twitch and jump as if it were alive.
Storyteller 3:	Do you know what I read? *(Confidentially)* Some scientists made a dead man quiver and open his eye. They did it—with electricity!
Storyteller 7:	*(Deep breath)* The breath of life—like Athena gave?
Storyteller 1:	Hardly! These were men of science and reason—and caution. Besides, it was against the law to use dead bodies that way.
Storyteller 3:	But just think what they imagined—what Mary imagined! *There's* a story!
Storyteller 1:	You're getting ahead. You're forgetting the evening when Mr. Godwin invited a really radical man to their house—Percy Bysshe Shelley—a poet full of wild ideas.
Storyteller 6:	Mary was—sixteen? And Shelley was a young man.
Storyteller 5:	Twenty-two years old and good-looking.
Storyteller 4:	Not like Coleridge, I bet—over forty and really pudgy!
Storyteller 6:	Imagine what Mary thought when she first saw him.
Mary:	Percy? *(Smiles)* Oh, he was a most esteemed and excellent person! *I* remember the evening. We all do! Percy swept into our house like a shower of sunlight.
Storyteller 1:	One friend wrote that Shelley . . . looked wild, intellectual, unearthly; like a spirit that has just descended from the sky; like a demon risen at that moment out of the ground.
Mary:	Oh, that's exactly right.
Storyteller 3:	And then? Then what happened?
Mary:	*(Takes a breath)* Ohhh.
Storyteller 2:	Let me guess. Sparks flew?
Mary:	Yes. I confess it.
Storyteller 4:	Was it electricity?
Storyteller 2:	I don't think so!
Mary:	Well, it was a little like that. We had so much in common. We both loved books, and we *had* to write. Most of all, we loved imagining wonderful things. But Father was not pleased. You see, Shelley wasn't exactly free. So we waited. We wrote to each other. Then we ran away—across the Channel to Paris.
Storyteller 4:	Just you and Shelley?
Mary:	And my half-sister, Claire. We three had a lovely time, but then our money ran out. We had to return to England. But we went back to Europe again—this time to the Alps in Switzerland. *(Shyly)* And this time with our little son, William.
Storyteller 3:	The Swiss mountains! *(Slight pause)* Did you go sightseeing?

Mary:	Oh, we intended to. But it proved a wet, ungenial summer, and incessant rain often confined us for days to the house. We made the best of it, however. We visited with our neighbor, Lord Byron. We read, we wrote, and we learned Greek for fun. But then, something mysterious happened.
Storyteller 1:	Go on. Tell us.
Mary:	Well, I was barely nineteen. The weather was perfectly dreadful, so we entertained ourselves, telling ghost stories at night—on and on, for hours and hours. Then *(Pause)* Lord Byron suggested we each write a ghost story. Percy and Lord Byron were very excited—but I never thought I could do it, until we began discussing—the elixir of life.
Storyteller 4:	The elixir—what is that?
Storyteller 1:	The elixir of life. The essential principle of life. The origin—the beginning—you know.
Mary:	Night after night we talked about it—the origin, the beginning of life. Suddenly, all that talk and all my reading and dreaming seemed to come together—to galvanize into one coherent thought.
Storyteller 3:	Well. And what did you do with that thought?
Mary:	I busied myself *to think of a* story—a story to . . . awaken thrilling horror—one to make the reader dread to look round, to curdle the blood, and quicken the beatings of the heart.
Storyteller 4:	So—you got an idea for a story?
Mary:	I did. I don't know how many days and nights it took. Finally, my imagination took hold. I had an idea.
Storyteller 3:	What would happen in your story?
Mary:	I thought—perhaps a corpse would be reanimated.
Storyteller 4:	A dead body reanimated? Brought back to life? How?
Mary:	*(Thoughtfully)* Galvanism had given token of such things. Experiments with electricity suggested such stimulation could make reanimation happen. I thought perhaps the component parts of a creature might be manufactured, brought together, and endowed with vital warmth.
Storyteller 2:	You're talking now about Prometheus making that clay figure and Athena giving it the breath of life!
Storyteller 3:	She's not talking myth; she's talking science. Her Prometheus is a scientist. He's a modern Prometheus who creates the monster.
Mary:	Exactly. But I needed a more modern name than just Prometheus. I needed something that would remind one of the mysterious Swiss Alps. So I named my Prometheus, my scientist, Frankenstein. Victor Frankenstein.
Storyteller 3:	Where is this scientist from—this Frankenstein?
Mary:	He will tell you. This is his book—his story.
Storyteller 1:	But it's a story he tells to someone else.
Mary:	Yes, to Robert Walton, captain of a sailing ship.

Storyteller 8:	And it's Captain Walton who then writes down the story in letters to his sister, back in England.
Storyteller 4:	Okay. *(Pause)* Okay—but what about the monster?
Mary:	That, too, is Frankenstein's story. You'll see. Start the first letter.
Storyteller 5:	I will: To Mrs. Saville. England. August 5th, 17—
Storyteller 1:	We don't have the year, but as Captain Walton writes—
Storyteller 7:	So strange an accident has happened to us that I cannot forbear recording it. Last Monday, July 31st, we were nearly surrounded by ice, which closed in the ship on all sides, scarcely leaving her the sea-room in which she floated.
Storyteller 3:	They're trapped—unable to move, like the ship in the *Ancient Mariner*. But in this story the ship is trapped by fog and snow and ice.
Storyteller 6:	About two o'clock . . . the mist cleared away, and we beheld, stretched out in every direction, vast and irregular plains of ice, which seemed to have no end.
Storyteller 1:	The men groaned, and the captain grew more anxious.
Storyteller 8:	When a strange sight suddenly attracted our attention. We perceived a low carriage, fixed on a sledge and drawn by dogs, pass on towards the north, at the distance of half a mile.
Storyteller 5:	A being which had the *shape* of a man—
Storyteller 6:	But apparently of *gigantic* stature—
Storyteller 5:	A being who sat in the sledge and guided the dogs. We . . . watched until he was lost among the distant inequalities of the ice.
Storyteller 7:	In the morning, however, as soon as it was light, I went upon deck and found all the sailors busy on one side of the vessel, apparently talking to someone in the sea.
Storyteller 8:	It was, in fact, a sledge, like that we had seen before, which had drifted towards us in the night.
Storyteller 7:	There was a human being within it . . . not a savage inhabitant of some undiscovered island, but a European.
Storyteller 8:	An exhausted man, Victor Frankenstein—who had come—
Storyteller 5:	*(Slowly)* "To seek the one who fled from me."
Storyteller 6:	Days passed. The exhausted man grew stronger. We are still surrounded by mountains of ice.
Storyteller 8:	The man then told me that he would commence his narrative the next day. . . . I have resolved . . . to record as nearly as possible . . . what he has related during the day. Even now, as I commence my task, his full-toned voice swells in my ears.
Storyteller 5:	I am by birth a Genevese.
Storyteller 7:	Ah, he's a Swiss, born and bred. And now another child, Elizabeth, joins the family to become his beautiful and adored companion.
Storyteller 5:	No human being could have passed a happier childhood.

Storyteller 8: However, he told the captain that even while growing up—

Storyteller 6: My temper was sometimes violent and my passions vehement; but by some law in my temperature they were turned not towards childish pursuits but to an eager desire to learn. . . . It was the secrets of heaven and earth that I desired to learn . . . the physical secrets of the world.

Storyteller 5: When I was about fifteen years old . . . we witnessed a most violent and terrible thunderstorm.

Storyteller 6: It advanced from behind the mountains . . . and the thunder burst at once with frightful loudness.

Storyteller 5: On a sudden I beheld a stream of fire issue from an old and beautiful oak . . . Soon as the dazzling light vanished, the oak had disappeared, and nothing remained but a blasted stump.

Storyteller 6: It was not splinted by the shock, but entirely reduced to thin ribbons of wood. I never beheld anything so utterly destroyed.

Storyteller 5: Soon after that experience with lightning, I heard the explanation of a theory . . . on the subject of electricity and galvanism . . . which disinclined me to pursue my accustomed studies.

Storyteller 6: All that had so long engaged my attention suddenly grew despicable. . . . I at once gave up my former occupations . . . and entertained the greatest disdain for a would-be science which could never even step within the threshold of real knowledge.

Storyteller 5: When I had attained the age of seventeen my parents resolved that I should become a student at the university of Ingolstadt.

Storyteller 6: Two years passed . . . engaged, heart and soul, in the pursuit of some discoveries which I hoped to make.

Storyteller 8: In other studies you go as far as others have gone before you, and there is nothing more to know; but in a scientific pursuit there is continual food for discovery and wonder.

Storyteller 5: One of the phenomena which had peculiarly attracted my attention was the structure of the human frame, and, indeed, any animal endued with life. Whence, I often asked myself, did the principle of life proceed? . . . To examine the causes of life, we must first have recourse to death. . . . The science of anatomy . . . was not sufficient. I must also observe the natural decay and corruption of the human body.

Storyteller 6: Darkness had no effect upon my fancy, and a churchyard . . . merely the receptacle of bodies deprived of life, which, from being the seat of beauty and strength, had become food for the worm.

Storyteller 5: Now I was forced to examine the cause and progress of this decay and forced to spend days and nights in vaults and charnel houses. After . . . incredible labour and fatigue, I succeeded in discovering the cause of generation and life; nay, more, I became myself capable of bestowing animation upon lifeless matter.

Storyteller 6: I began the creation of a human being . . . a gigantic structure, that is to say, about eight feet in height, and proportionably large.

Storyteller 5: In a solitary chamber, or rather cell, at the top of the house, and separated from all the other apartments by a gallery and staircase, I kept my workshop of filthy creation.

Storyteller 6: The dissecting room and the slaughter-house furnished many of my materials; and often did my human nature turn with loathing from my occupation, whilst, still urged on by an eagerness which perpetually increased, I brought my work near to a conclusion.

Storyteller 5: It was on a dreary night of November that I beheld the accomplishment of my toils.

Storyteller 8: With an anxiety that almost amounted to agony, I collected the instruments of life around me, that I might infuse a spark of being into the lifeless thing that lay at my feet.

Storyteller 3: Electricity—for the elixir of life!

Storyteller 2: Sssh! Sssh! *(Whispers)* It's the breath of life—like Athena!

Storyteller 6: *(Slowly)* It was already one in the morning; the rain pattered dismally against the panes, and my candle was nearly burnt out—

Storyteller 7: *(Slowly)* When by the glimmer of the half-extinguished light, I saw the dull yellow eye of the creature open; it breathed hard, and a convulsive motion agitated its limbs.

Storyteller 8: How can I describe my emotions at this catastrophe, or how delineate the wretch whom with such infinite pains and care I had endeavored to form?

Storyteller 5: His limbs were in proportion, and I had selected his features as beautiful.

Storyteller 6: Beautiful? His yellow skin scarcely covered the work of muscles and arteries beneath; his hair was of a lustrous black, and flowing; his teeth of a pearly whiteness; but these luxuriances only formed a more horrid contrast with his watery eyes—

Storyteller 7: Eyes that seemed almost of the same colour as the dun-white sockets in which they were set, his shriveled complexion and straight black lips.

Storyteller 8: The different accidents of life are not so changeable as the feelings of human nature. I had worked hard for nearly two years, for the sole purpose of infusing life into an inanimate body. For this I had deprived myself of rest and health . . .

Storyteller 7: But now that I had finished, the beauty of the dream vanished, and breathless horror and disgust filled my heart.

Storyteller 8: Unable to bear the aspect of the being I had created, I rushed out of the room and continued a long time traversing my bed-chamber, unable to compose my mind to sleep.

Storyteller 5: At length lassitude succeeded to the tumult I had before endured, and I threw myself on the bed in my clothes, endeavoring to seek a few moments of forgetfulness. But it was in vain.

Storyteller 7: I slept, indeed, but I was disturbed by the wildest dreams. I thought I saw Elizabeth, in the bloom of health, walking in the streets of Ingolstadt.

Storyteller 8: Delighted and surprised, I embraced her, but as I imprinted the first kiss on her lips, they became livid with the hue of death; her features appeared to change, and I thought I held the corpse of my dead mother in my arms.

Storyteller 6: *(Whispers)* A shroud enveloped her form. . . . *(Slowly)* And I saw the grave-worms crawling in the folds of the flannel.

Storyteller 5: I started from my sleep with horror; a cold dew covered my forehead, my teeth chattered, and every limb became convulsed.

Storyteller 6: When, by the dim and yellow light of the moon, as it forced its way through the window shutters, I beheld the wretch—the miserable monster whom I had created.

Storyteller 7: He held up the curtain of the bed; and his eyes, if eyes they may be called, were fixed on me.

Storyteller 8: His jaws opened, and he muttered some inarticulate sounds, while a grin wrinkled his cheeks.

Storyteller 6: He might have spoken, but I did not hear.

Storyteller 5: One hand was stretched out, seemingly to detain me.

Storyteller 6: But I escaped and rushed downstairs.

Storyteller 8: I took refuge in the courtyard . . . where I remained during the rest of the night, walking up and down in the greatest agitation, listening attentively, catching and fearing each sound as if it were to announce the approach of the demoniacal corpse to which I had so miserably given life.

Storyteller 7: I passed the night wretchedly. . . . Dreams that had been my food and pleasant rest for so long a space were now become a hell to me; and the change was so rapid, the overthrow so complete!

Storyteller 6: Morning, dismal and wet, at length dawned. I issued into the streets without any clear conception of where I was or what I was doing.

Storyteller 5: My heart palpitated in the sickness of fear, and I hurried on with irregular steps, not daring to look bout me.

Storyteller 6: But remembering, remembering Coleridge and the albatross that haunted the ancient mariner—now Frankenstein has *his* frightful fiend that would not go away.

(Storytellers read the following verse slowly, like a dirge)

Storyteller 5: Like one who, on a lonely road,

Storyteller 6: Doth walk in fear and dread,

Storyteller 7: And, having once turned round,

Storyteller 5: Walks on,

Storyteller 6: And turns no more his head;

Storyteller 7: Because he knows—

Storyteller 8: A frightful fiend
Doth close behind him tread.

**Storytellers
5, 6, 7, 8:** *(Whisper slowly in unison)*
A frightful fiend
Doth
Close behind him
Tread.

(All Storytellers close folders and bow their heads as Announcer enters to center stage)

Announcer: The monster does not give up. He's almost human. He has feelings—loneliness, despair, anger, then—revenge! He kills, then kills again, and then again. Frankenstein goes after his monster. He follows him all the way to the frozen north. The sailors on that ship see him. But does Frankenstein ever find him? *(Pause)* Or is the monster still alive, out there, frozen in the ice? *(Announcer holds up a copy of* Frankenstein*)* Hey, you might want to check it out! *(All bow and Announcer exits)*

Robert Louis Stevenson, Tusitala, Spins
Treasure Island

The natives of Samoa called him Tusitala, Teller of Tales, and they honored him as an island chieftain. The rest of the world knew him as Robert Louis Stevenson, the brilliant author of such diverse writings as travel books, political essays, *A Child's Garden of Verses*, *Doctor Jekyll and Mr. Hyde*, *Kidnapped*, and the adventure story for all time—*Treasure Island*.

Born in Edinburgh, Scotland, in 1850, Stevenson was expected to follow the family tradition and become a civil engineer. Instincts and aspirations aside, that work proved to be too difficult for a young man already plagued with a lung disease. Consequently, he entered Edinburgh University and studied law. He never practiced. He wanted to become a writer.

Seeking mild climates for his health, he spent much of the early 1870s abroad and began to write. While living in France, he fell in love with Fanny Osbourne, an older American woman with two children and estranged from her husband. Although she returned home, this match seemed meant to be. Stevenson traveled clear across America to see her, and they married in 1880.

Unfortunately, Stevenson's tuberculosis directed much of the course of their lives. They traveled widely, seeking a cure or a respite from his disease. Still, his stories poured out—and *Treasure Island*, written for his young stepson, soon made him famous.

Finally, in 1890, they settled in Samoa, built a house, and entered into the lives of the native people. Stevenson continued to write, but in 1894 he died—too young, but leaving a bright legacy of classic tales, such as the adventure novel *Treasure Island*.

Presentation of Robert Louis Stevenson Script

The classic tale of *Treasure Island* is chock full of vivid descriptions, colorful language, and a plot to make the pages fly. Thus, it will be easy for young readers to bring these elements alive in a spirited readers theatre production of Stevenson's famous adventure.

The story is narrated by the young hero, Jim Hawkins. Exciting scenes abound with his mentors, the doctor and the squire, and the pirates—the chief villain being, of course, Long John Silver. It is a great story for readers to have fun with.

Because the hero, Jim Hawkins, is such a dominant character, this script divides up his lines with the device of using Jim 1 and Jim 2. (It is possible, of course, to combine these lines into only one Jim.) The present script calls for a cast of fifteen.

Treasure Island has only one female character in the book—Jim's mother. The Announcer and the parts of Storytellers 1, 2, 3, and 4 are also suitable for girls. All other parts, readers 6 through 12, depict male characters.

Stage Props

14 reading stands, if possible

14 tall stools or chairs

Hand Props

15 scripts (plus 1 for the teacher)

15 black folders for scripts

Robert Louis Stevenson, Tusitala, Spins *Treasure Island*

Production note: Key to staging—Jim 1 and Jim 2; Storytellers l, 2, 3, 4; Mother, 5; Doctor, 6; Parrot, 7; Squire, 8; Black Dog, 9; Captain, 10; Blind Man, 11; Long John, 12.

```
                        X   X
                      Jim 1 Jim 2
        X  X  X  X                        X  X    X
        1  2  3  4                        5  6    7
                                        X  X  X  X  X
                                        8  9 10 11 12

                          Announcer
```

—◄◆►—

Announcer:	*(Takes center stage)* Welcome, friends, to Storyteller Theatre, where classic authors and their works come alive. "How?" you may ask. And the answer—with our readers extraordinaire!
Storyteller 4:	I'm impressed already!
Announcer:	Impressed is good. Excited is better—for today's story is an adventure tale full of narrow escapes, hidden treasure, and dastardly pirates. Our classic storyteller is Robert Louis Stevenson, and his book is—
Storyteller 3:	*Treasure Island*!
Storyteller 2:	*Treasure Island*? Hey, my dad read that.
Storyteller 3:	I'll bet my granddad read that.
Storyteller 4:	I saw the movie.
Storyteller 2:	My dad saw the movie of *Treasure Island* when he was a kid.
Announcer:	And your granddad saw it, too. Right? I think we get the idea. Famous book from 1883. Made into a movie three times. It's a classic! But have you read it? Really dipped into the adventures of our hero, Jim Hawkins? *(Pause)* Ah, maybe not. Now you can. It's Jim Hawkins who tells the story—and for us *(Indicates)* two Jims to tell the story and *(Indicates)* eight characters within.
Storyteller 2:	And we can tell about it. Okay?
Announcer:	Okay—I guess. For now, let's set our sails and cast off for our adventure to *Treasure Island*! Jim—begin! *(Bows and exits)*
Jim 1:	I take up my pen . . . and go back to the time when my father kept the Admiral Benbow inn, and the brown old seaman, with the sabre cut, first took up lodging under our roof.
Storyteller 3:	Right off you can tell this book is going to move with the sea.
Storyteller 1:	Certainly. The inn is named for a British admiral who fought a fierce battle with the French in the West Indies.

Storyteller 4:	Stevenson must have had dreams about those faraway islands.
Storyteller 1:	Lush, warm, lazy living—why wouldn't it appeal to him? He came from Edinburgh, Scotland, born and educated there—near the sea, all right, but not a good climate for anyone with lung disease.
Storyteller 3:	We're talking mid-1800s? I bet it was tuberculosis.
Storyteller 1:	And you'd be right. Horrible disease. Hard to breathe. Stevenson spent most of his life looking for a better climate to help his lungs.
Storyteller 3:	I'd try the south of France. That's not too far from Scotland.
Storyteller 1:	He spent many winters in France—some in Italy, some Belgium.
Storyteller 2:	That would take money. How did he survive—you know, work?
Storyteller 1:	His parents helped. His father was a civil engineer and wanted his son to be one, too. But the work was too strenuous. So being a dutiful son, he studied law, but never practiced the law. You see, he really wanted to be a writer!
Storyteller 2:	Is it possible to make a lot of money writing? Could Stevenson?
Storyteller 1:	He didn't at first. He wrote travel stories and essays and poems and short stories, but he didn't become really famous or really make much money until he wrote—
Storyteller 3:	*Treasure Island*! I'm just guessing, but a classic like that—
Storyteller 2:	I get it. Success big time! But then what?
Storyteller 1:	No stopping him. He wrote *Treasure Island* for his stepson. But have you also heard of *Kidnapped*? *Doctor Jekyll and Mr. Hyde*?
Storyteller 4:	Too scary. The good guy with that horrible side to him. Scary.
Storyteller 3:	Like two sides of a coin. Like the pirate, Long John Silver.
Storyteller 2:	His parrot's always screeching, "Pieces of eight. Pieces of eight."
Storyteller 3:	The old Spanish peso—a silver coin with two different sides. Long John has two sides to him, too. Is that a coincidence or not?
Storyteller 1:	Stevenson had a theory: "In a bad man may be all the machinery to be a good one, made useless by the malady of not wanting."
Storyteller 2:	That's heavy! The bad guy could be good if he wanted to? What about "the brown old seaman, with the sabre cut" who seeks lodging at the Admiral Benbow? What does Jim say about him?
Jim 1:	I remember him as if it were yesterday, as he came plodding to the inn door, his sea-chest following behind him in a hand-barrow.
Jim 2:	A tall, strong, heavy, nut-brown man; his tarry pigtail falling over the shoulders of his soiled blue coat; his hands ragged and scarred, with black, broken nails; and the sabre cut across one cheek, a dirty, livid white. I remember him looking around the cove and whistling to himself . . . and then breaking out in that old sea-song:
Captain:	*Fifteen men on the Dead Man's Chest—* *Yo-ho-ho, and a bottle of rum!* This is a handy cove. . . . Help up my chest. . . . I'll stay here a bit. I'm a plain man; rum and bacon and eggs is what I want, and that head up there for to watch the ships off. *(Laughs)* And you mought call me captain.

Jim 2: All day he hung around the cove, or upon the cliffs, with a brass telescope. . . . Every day, when he came back from his stroll, he would ask if any seafaring men had gone along the road. . . . He had taken me aside one day, and promised me a silver fourpenny on the first of every month if I would only keep my weather-eye open for *(Slowly)* a seafaring man with one leg.

Jim 1: How that personage haunted my dreams, I need scarcely tell you. On stormy nights, when the wind shook the four corners of the house, and the surf roared along the cove and up the cliffs, I would see him in a thousand forms, and with a thousand diabolical expressions.

Jim 2: Now the leg would be cut off at the knee, now at the hip; now he was a monstrous kind of a creature who had never had but the one leg, and that in the middle of his body. To see him leap and run and pursue me over hedge and ditch was the worst of nightmares.

Jim 1: But then—one January morning, very early—a pinching, frosty morning—the cove all grey with hoar-frost, the ripple lapping softly on the stones, the sun still low and only touching the hilltops and shining far to seaward . . . the parlour door opened, and a man stepped in on whom I had never set my eyes before.

Jim 2: He was a pale, tallowy creature, wanting two fingers of the left hand; and, though he wore a cutlass, he did not look much like a fighter. I had always my eye open for seafaring men, with one leg or two, and I remember this one puzzled me.

Storyteller 2: What's he want—wearing that sword? Bet he's up to no good.

Jim 1: The stranger kept hanging about just inside the inn door, peering round the corner like a cat waiting for a mouse. . . . At last in strode the captain, and the strange creature spoke to him.

Black Dog: Bill!

Jim 2: The captain spun round . . . and fronted us; all the brown had gone out of his face, and even his nose was blue; he had the look of a man who sees a ghost, or the evil one, or something worse.

Black Dog: Come, Bill, you know me; you know an old shipmate, Bill.

Jim 1: The captain made a sort of gasp.

Captain: Black Dog!

Black Dog: And who else? Black Dog as ever was, come for to see his old shipmate Billy. . . . Ah, Bill, Bill, we have seen a sight of times, us two, since I lost them two talons.

Jim 1: He held up his mutilated hand.

Storyteller 4: Oh, no! What then? What did he want?

Jim 2: They began to quarrel. Then all of a sudden there was a tremendous explosion of oaths and other noises—the chair and table went over in a lump, a clash of steel followed, and then a cry of pain, and the next instant I saw Black Dog in full flight, and the captain hotly pursuing, both with drawn cutlasses, and the former streaming blood from the left shoulder.

Jim 1: That blow was the last of the battle. Once out upon the road, Black Dog, in spite of his wound . . . disappeared in half a minute.

Storyteller 2:	I know! Then the captain calls for rum, but Doctor Livesey warns him—no more rum or he'll die of a stroke.
Captain:	That doctor's a fool, I tell you. If I don't have a drain o' rum, Jim, I'll have the horrors. . . . A golden guinea for a noggin, Jim.
Jim 2:	*(To the captain)* I want none of your money, but what you owe my father. I'll get you one glass, and no more. *(Back briefly)* When I brought it to him, he seized it greedily, and drank it out.
Captain:	Jim, you saw that seafaring man today?
Jim 2:	Black Dog?
Captain:	Ah, Black Dog. . . . *He's* a bad 'un; but there's worse that put him on. Now, if I can't get away nohow, and they tip me the black spot, mind you, it's my old sea-chest they're after. . . . I was . . . old Flint's first mate, and I'm the on'y one as knows the place. . . . But you won't peach unless they get the black spot on me, or unless you see that Black Dog again, or a seafaring man with one leg, Jim—him above all.
Jim 2:	But what is the black spot, Captain?
Captain:	That's a summons, mate. I'll tell you if they get that.
Storyteller 3:	This is getting very confusing. What is the black spot—a summons to what? And what's in that mysterious sea chest?
Storyteller 1:	Patience, friend. The plot thickens!
Jim 1:	About three o'clock of a bitter, foggy, frosty afternoon, I was standing at the door for a moment . . . when I saw someone drawing slowly near along the road.
Jim 2:	He was plainly blind, for he tapped before him with a stick, and wore a great green shade over his eyes and nose; and he was hunched, as if with age or weakness, and wore a huge old tattered sea-cloak with a hood, that made him appear positively deformed.
Jim 1:	I never saw in my life a more dreadful looking figure. He stopped a little from the inn, and raising his voice in an odd sing-song, addressed the air in front of him:
Blind Man:	Will any kind friend inform a poor blind man, who has lost the precious sight of his eyes in the gracious defence of his native country, England, and God bless King George!—where or in what part of this country he may now be?
Jim 1:	You are at the Admiral Benbow, Black Hill Cove, my good man.
Blind Man:	I hear a voice—a young voice. Will you give me your hand, my kind, young friend, and lead me in?
Jim 1:	I held out my hand, and the horrible, soft-spoken, eyeless creature gripped it in a moment like a vice. I was so much startled that I struggled to withdraw; but the blind man pulled me close up to him with a single action of his arm.
Blind Man:	Now, boy, take me in to the captain.
Jim 1:	Sir, upon my word I dare not.
Blind Man:	*(Sneering)* Oh, that's it! Take me in straight, or I'll break your arm.
Jim 1:	And he gave it, as he spoke, a wrench that made me cry out. . . . The blind man clung close to me, holding me in one iron fist. . . . And as I opened the parlour

door . . . the poor captain raised his eyes, and at one look the rum went out of him, and left him staring sober. The expression of his face was not so much of terror as of mortal sickness.

Blind Man: Now, Bill, sit where you are. . . . Boy, take his left hand by the wrist, and bring it near to my right.

Jim 1: I obeyed him to the letter, and I saw him pass something from the hollow of the hand that held his stick into the palm of the captain's, which closed upon it instantly.

Blind Man: And now that's done.

Jim 2: And at the words he suddenly left hold of me, and with incredible accuracy and nimbleness, skipped out of the parlour and into the road, where, as I still stood motionless, I could hear his stick go tap-tap-tapping into the distance.

Jim 1: The captain drew in his hand and looked sharply into the palm.

Captain: Ten o'clock!

Jim 2: He sprang to his feet. Even as he did so, he reeled, put his hand to his throat, stood swaying for a moment, and then, with a peculiar sound, fell from his whole height face foremost to the floor.

Jim 1: I ran to him at once, calling to my mother. But haste was all in vain. The captain had been struck dead by thundering apoplexy.

Mother: Oh, no, Jim. No!

Jim 2: It seemed impossible for either of us to remain much longer in the house: the fall of coals in the kitchen grate, the very ticking of the clock, filled us with alarms. . . . And what between the dead body of the captain on the parlour floor, and the thought of that detestable blind beggar hovering near at hand, and ready to return, there were moments when, as the saying goes, I jumped in my skin for terror.

Jim 1: It occurred to us to . . . seek help in the neighboring hamlet. . . . But the name of Captain Flint . . . carried a great weight of terror. . . . Not one would help us to defend the inn against these strangers.

Jim 2: My mother made our neighbors a speech. She would not, she declared, lose money that belonged to her fatherless boy.

Mother: If none of the rest of you dare, Jim and I dare. Back we will go, the way we came, and small thanks to you big, hulking, chicken-hearted men. We'll have that chest open, if we die for it.

Jim 2: We left them and returned to the inn. I slipped the bolt at once, and we stood and panted for a moment in the dark, alone in the house with the dead captain's body, not knowing who was without.

Jim 1: Then my mother got a candle in the bar, and, holding each other's hands, we advanced into the parlour. *(Pause)* He lay as we had left him, on his back, with his eyes open, and one arm stretched out.

Mother: *(Whispering)* Draw down the blind, Jim. . . . They might come and watch outside. . . . We have to get the key off *that*; and who's to touch it I should like to know!

Jim 2:	She gave a kind of sob. I went down on my knees at once. On the floor close to his hand there was a little round of paper, blackened on the one side. I could not doubt that this was the *black spot*.
Mother:	Now, Jim, that key . . . perhaps it's round his neck.
Jim 2:	Overcoming a strong repugnance, I tore open his shirt at the neck, and there, sure enough, hanging to a bit of tarry string, which I cut with his own gully, we found the key.
Jim 1:	We hurried upstairs, without delay, to the little room . . . where his box had stood since the day of his arrival.
Mother:	Jim. Jim! Give me the key.
Jim 2:	Though the lock was very stiff, she had turned it and thrown back the lid in a twinkling. The miscellany began.
Jim 1:	We had found nothing of any value . . . until there lay before us, the last things in the chest, a bundle tied up in oilcloth, and looking like papers, and a canvas bag, that gave forth, at a touch, the jingle of gold.
Storyteller 3:	I get it. Jim's mother takes enough money to pay for the dead captain's bill. But what's tied up in the oilcloth?
Storyteller 2:	Has to be something valuable. The captain had kept it hidden, and those two—Black Dog and the blind man—were sure after it.
Storyteller 1:	You're right. So Jim leaves his mother at the inn to take the oilskin packet to Dr. Livesey and Squire Trelawney for safekeeping.
Jim 2:	The doctor opened the seals with great care, and there fell out the map of an island, with . . . every particular that would be needed to bring a ship to a safe anchorage upon its shores.
Storyteller 1:	Not surprising. Stevenson knew all about maps. He'd made many trips across the English Channel. He'd crossed the Atlantic. Easy for him to imagine, to draw, the shape of Treasure Island.
Jim 2:	It was about nine miles long and five across, shaped, you might say, like a fat dragon standing up, and had two fine land-locked harbours, and a hill in the center part marked The Spy-glass.
Jim 1:	But, above all, three crosses of red ink—two on the north part of the island, one in the south-west, and, beside this last, in the same red ink, and in a small, neat hand . . . these words: *(Slowly)* Bulk of treasure here.
Storyteller 2:	That must have thrilled Jim Hawkins.
Storyteller 1:	And the squire and Dr. Livesey. The squire burst with delight:
Squire:	Livesey, you will give up this wretched practice at once. Tomorrow I start for Bristol. In three weeks' time—three weeks!—two weeks—ten days—we'll have the best ship, sir, and the choicest crew in England. Hawkins shall come as cabin-boy. You'll make a famous cabin-boy, Hawkins. You, Livesey are ship's doctor; I am admiral. . . . We'll have favourable winds, a quick passage, and not the least difficulty in finding the spot, and money to eat—to roll in . . . ever after.
Doctor:	Trelawney, I'll go with you . . . so will Jim, and, be a credit to the undertaking. There's only one man I'm afraid of.

Squire:	And who's that? Name the dog, sir!
Doctor:	You, for you cannot hold your tongue. We are not the only men who know of this paper. . . . From first to last, not one of us must breathe a word of what we've found.
Squire:	Livesey, you are always in the right of it. I'll be silent as the grave.
Jim 1:	It was longer than the squire imagined ere we were ready for the sea. . . . So the weeks passed on, till there came a letter addressed to Dr. Livesey from the squire working in Bristol seaport—but talking *(Pause)* most unwisely about their sailing for treasure.
Squire:	The ship is bought and fitted. She lies at anchor, ready for sea. You never imagined a sweeter schooner—a child might sail her—two hundred tons; name, *Hispaniola*. . . . So far there was not a hitch. . . . It was the crew that troubled me . . . till the most remarkable stroke of fortune brought me the very man I required. I found he was an old sailor, kept a public-house, knew all the sea-faring men in Bristol, had lost his health ashore, and wanted a good berth as cook to get to sea again. . . . I engaged him on the spot. . . . Long John Silver, he is called, and has lost a leg.
Jim 2:	The squire's letter finished with "Seaward, ho! Hang the treasure!"
Squire:	It's the glory of the sea that has turned my head. So now, Livesey, come post; do not lose an hour. . . . Let young Hawkins go at once to see his mother . . . then both come with full speed to Bristol.
Jim 2:	Once I arrived in Bristol, the squire gave me a note addressed to John Silver, at the sign of the Spy-glass, and told me I should easily find the place by following the line of the docks and keeping a bright look-out for a little tavern with a large brass telescope for sign. I set off . . . and picked my way among a great crowd of people . . . until I found the tavern in question. While I was waiting, a man came out of a side room, and, at a glance, I was sure he must be Long John. His left leg was cut off close by the hip, and under the left shoulder he carried a crutch, which he managed with wonderful dexterity, hopping about on it like a bird.
Jim 1:	He was very tall and strong, with a face as big as a ham—plain and pale, but intelligent and smiling. . . . To tell you the truth, from the very first mention of Long John in Squire Trewlaney's letter, I had taken a fear in my mind that he might prove to be the very one-legged sailor whom I watched for so long at the old Benbow.
Jim 2:	But one look at the man before me was enough. I had seen the captain, and Black Dog, and the blind man Pew, and I thought I knew what a buccaneer was like—a very different creature, according to me, from this clean and pleasant-tempered landlord.
Jim 1:	But to tell the truth, I was not alone in trusting Long John Silver.
Doctor:	Well, squire, I don't put much faith in your discoveries, as a general thing; but I will say this, John Silver suits me.
Squire:	*(Enthusiastically)* The man's a perfect trump.
Jim 2:	All the crew respected and even obeyed him. He had a way of talking to each, and doing everybody some particular service.

Jim 1:	To me he was unweariedly kind; and always glad to see me in the galley, which he kept as clean as a new pin; the dishes hanging up burnished, and his parrot in a cage in one corner. Friendly, always!
Long John:	Come away, Hawkins. Come and have a yarn with John. Nobody more welcome than yourself, my son. Sit you down and hear the news. *(Indicates)* Here's Cap'n Flint—I calls my parrot Cap'n Flint, after the famous buccaneer—here's Cap'n Flint predicting success to our v'yage. Wasn't you, cap'n?
Parrot:	*(Rapidly)* Pieces of eight! Pieces of eight! Pieces of eight!
Long John:	Ah, she's a handsome craft, she is. . . . Here's this poor old innocent bird o' mine swearing blue fire, and none the wiser, you may lay to that. She would swear the same, in a manner of speaking, before chaplain.
Jim 1:	And John would touch his forelock with a solemn way he had, that made me think he was the best of men.
Storyteller 1:	Until one night—when Jim thought he should like an apple.
Jim 1:	I ran on deck. The watch was all forward looking out for the island. The man at the helm was . . . whistling away gently to himself; and that was the only sound except the swish of the sea against the bows and around the sides of the ship.
Jim 2:	In I got bodily into the apple barrel, and found there was scarce an apple left, but, sitting down there in the dark, what with the sound of the waters and the rocking movement of the ship, I had either fallen asleep, or was on the point of doing so, when a heavy man sat down with a clash close by.
Jim 1:	The barrel shook as he leaned his shoulders against it, and I was just about to jump up when the man began to speak.
Jim 2:	It was Silver's voice.
Jim 1:	Before I had heard a dozen words, I would not have shown myself for all the world, but lay there, trembling and listening, in the extreme of fear and curiosity; for from these dozen words I understood that the lives of all the honest men aboard depended upon me alone.
Storyteller 1:	Silver and his pirates are making plans to take over the ship.
Storyteller 3:	What will happen to the crew—the doctor, the squire—to Jim!
Storyteller 1:	Doesn't sound good. One man tells Silver, "Dead men don't bite."
Long John:	Right you are—rough and ready. But mark you here: I'm an easy man—I'm quite the gentleman, says you; but this time it's serious. Dooty is dooty, mates. I give my vote—death. . . . Cross me, and you'll go where many a good man's gone before you, first and last . . . some to the yard-arm, shiver my timbers! and some by the board, and all to feed the fishes.
Storyteller 2:	Flip that coin! What can Jim Hawkins do now?
Storyteller 1:	Read on! Remember, Robert Louis Stevenson loved adventures. Exciting, romantic adventures poured right out of him.
Storyteller 4:	He was romantic, all right—the way he pursued Fanny Osbourne.
Storyteller 2:	A married lady—an American lady—with two children.

Storyteller 4:	They met in France. He was traveling and writing. She was traveling, too, but unhappy, already separating from her husband.
Storyteller 3:	So they met in France, married, and lived happily ever after?
Storyteller 1:	Not until she returned to California and was free—divorced. Then, to persuade her, Stevenson crossed the Atlantic, then the whole U.S. continent by train. Not an easy trip in those days—1879.
Storyteller 3:	And it was for her son, Lloyd, that he wrote *Treasure Island*?
Storyteller 2:	Yes. Then more stories, more novels—some written with Lloyd. But that shadow of tuberculosis hung over the whole little family. The search for a cure, for the right climate, continued.
Storyteller 1:	They returned to Europe—tried Switzerland. Not right. The French Riviera, the seacoast of England, Scotland, London. Finally they came back to America, and Stevenson tried a health resort for tubercular patients in the Adirondack Mountains of New York.
Storyteller 4:	He's still writing—novels, articles, short stories. But still ill.
Storyteller 1:	Then after almost a year in America, Stevenson and his family took a long cruise through the South Pacific. Nothing satisfied them like their visit to Samoa. In November 1890, they settled in Samoa, and Stevenson built a house.
Storyteller 3:	On his own Treasure Island! Sounds like Paradise.
Storyteller 1:	He was happy, healthier, and became part of the island's affairs.
Storyteller 4:	I know. He actually became sort of an island chieftain.
Storyteller 2:	What was it the islanders called him? Tusitala—Teller of Tales.
Storyteller 3:	And of poetry, too. Remember? "The world is so full of a number of things, I'm sure we should all be as happy as kings." Talk about positive thinking!
Storyteller 2:	He had to be an optimist. "Am I no a bonny fighter?" he wrote.
Storyteller 1:	But at age forty-four, in 1894, Stevenson died. He was buried with all the honors and ceremony due a chieftain, on top of a mountain, thirteen hundred feet above the Pacific. Tusitala was gone.
Announcer:	*(Enters stage right)* But we remember him well—with more fondness than Jim Hawkins remembers his adventure to Treasure Island. The pirates, the escapes, the many deaths stay with him to the bitter end.
Jim 1:	Oxen and wain-ropes would not bring me back again to that accursed island.
Jim 2:	And the worst dreams that ever I have are when I hear the surf booming about its coasts, or start upright in bed, with the sharp voice of Captain Flint still ringing in my ears:
Parrot:	Pieces of eight! Pieces of eight!
Storytellers All:	*(Softly, slowly, as an echo)* Pieces of eight! Pieces of eight!
Announcer:	*(To center stage)* So be off with you! It's *Treasure Island* by Robert Louis Stevenson that you want—a true classic bound to shiver your timbers!

The Path to *Uncle Tom's Cabin* with Harriet Beecher Stowe

Uncle Tom's Cabin, or Life among the Lowly offers modern readers a classic example of the power of the pen. Harriet Beecher Stowe, who wielded that pen, became beloved, maligned, admired, and scorned for the passion behind that pen.

The book, enormously popular from the outset, may seem quaint, outdated, even maudlin today. Yet it demonstrates the strength of emotional writing when logic and reason alone are unable to change the hearts and minds of people.

In 1811 Harriet Beecher, the seventh child of Roxana and the illustrious Reverend Dr. Lyman Beecher, was born in Litchfield, Connecticut. When little Hattie was five years old, her gentle, artistic mother died. Raised by an older sister, Catherine, by aunts, her grandmother, and then her stepmother, the young precocious girl gravitated to the intellect and charm of her father and brothers. Later, her husband, Calvin Stowe, would become her strongest love and support. Seven children of that marriage soon more than filled her life.

Samuel Johnson, that brilliant literary man of the 1700s from Litchfield, England, pronounced famously that "No man but a blockhead ever wrote, except for money." But that statement barely touches the literary and emotional drive that spurred the work of Harriet Beecher Stowe. She was a woman who understood her own talent. She understood the need to use it—both to earn money and to satisfy her urge to write.

A born storyteller who early on called for "a room of her own," Harriet Beecher Stowe, at age forty-one, brought her intellect, her sensitivity, and her skill to her one memorable book, *Uncle Tom's Cabin*, and she moved the world.

Presentation of Harriet Beecher Stowe Script

Try as we may, sometimes we can't dismiss the often tormented heritage that lies behind the foundation of our country. Books remind us of that. Styles change, words evolve, attitudes come and go. Authors of the past—Chaucer, Shakespeare, Dickens, Twain, and Harriet Beecher Stowe—remind us of where we have been and how far we have come. *Uncle Tom's Cabin, or Life among the Lowly* is one famous book that prods our memory.

Stowe, like Dickens and Twain, experimented with the language of dialects. For example, in *Uncle Tom's Cabin*, Haley uses *ar* for are and *onpleasant* for unpleasant, and Eva says "everybody else *call* me Eva." In addition, we might call the spelling and punctuation here creative. Such authentic, unusual qualities are preserved in this script.

The readers theatre script calls for seventeen readers, including the Announcer. The parts of Storytellers 3 and 5 are probably best read by girls. The Announcer can be read by either a girl or a boy.

When the performance begins, readers will make their entrance and stand in front of their chairs. They sit, one by one, as the Announcer introduces them.

Stage Props

16 reading stands, if possible

16 tall stools or chairs

Hand Props

17 scripts (plus 1 for the teacher)

17 black folders for scripts

1 copy of *Uncle Tom's Cabin* for Announcer to show title at end of show

The Path to *Uncle Tom's Cabin* with Harriet Beecher Stowe

X X X X X
1 2 3 4 5

Catherine Dr. Beecher   Eliza George Legree
X   X   X   X   X

Charles   Harriet   Haley Shelby   Eva Tom
X   X   X   X   X   X

Announcer

——◆◆◆——

Announcer:	*(Enters to center stage)* Welcome to Storyteller Theatre and the remarkable world of Harriet Beecher Stowe—a storyteller who shook the world! The influence of her novel *Uncle Tom's Cabin* just grew and grew until even President Abraham Lincoln acknowledged its power. *(Pause)* Ah, but that's part of the story. Let me introduce our characters for today. *(Each sits on cue)* First and foremost, Harriet Beecher Stowe; her son, Charles; her sister, Catherine; and her father, Dr. Lyman Beecher. Then—our five Storytellers, ready to present her book, so that you may meet her characters: Mr. Haley, Mr. Shelby, Eliza, George, Simon Legree, Eva, and, of course, Uncle Tom. Now, let's begin. I think you'll be impressed! *(Announcer exits)*
Storyteller 1:	Well, to begin with, let's set the time. Charles? You're her son.
Charles:	How about 1811—the year my mother was born? My grandfather can speak to that occasion.
Dr. Beecher:	She was a tiny thing, our seventh child, but like I told her mother, little Hattie was full of life. *(Pause, then firmly)* Only, I wish she'd been born a boy.
Charles:	That's my grandfather, all right—the Reverend Dr. Lyman Beecher. When my mother was growing up, Grandfather Beecher was the most famous preacher in America. He was known to have very strong opinions. And he spoke his mind—generally about religion, though. Isn't that right, Mother?
Harriet:	Now, Charles, be fair. Father wished I'd been a boy so that I could be a preacher. Girls couldn't become preachers in my day.
Charles:	But you became a writer and made him proud.
Harriet:	I did try—from the time I was a little girl.
Charles:	And won the essay contest at eleven?
Harriet:	Yes. When mine was read . . . father . . . brightened and looked interested, and at the close I heard him ask—
Dr. Beecher:	Who wrote that composition?
Storyteller 1:	And they told him, "Your daughter, sir!"

Harriet:	It was the proudest moment of my life. There was no mistaking father's face when he was pleased. But I always knew, you see, he wanted sons to carry on his work.
Storyteller 2:	He produced a good many sons, I understand.
Harriet:	*(Laughs)* Oh, he did. *(Seriously)* And my brothers were all preachers at one time in their lives. My younger brother, the Reverend Henry Ward, became every bit as famous as Father.
Charles:	That may be, Mother, but it's your name that people remember—especially because of one book that you wrote.
Harriet:	Ah, yes—*Uncle Tom's Cabin.* But the fame is not mine, Charles. I did not write that book.
Charles:	Mother, perhaps you'd better explain that.
Harriet:	It was by God's hand, not mine. He wrote that book.
Storyteller 3:	*Uncle Tom's Cabin* is a religious book?
Storyteller 5:	I don't think it's a religious book.
Storyteller 4:	Of course it is. All the good characters live according to the Golden Rule. Doesn't that tell you something?
Storyteller 3:	And the bad characters?
Storyteller 4:	Well, they don't follow the Golden Rule. They haven't a clue what it means. "Do unto others as you would have them do unto you?" They could care less!
Charles:	Right! And look at the trouble that attitude causes. Take that man, Haley, at the very beginning of mother's book.
Storyteller 2:	Haley? Now there's a really bad character. He buys people and sells them again—like he does with Uncle Tom.
Charles:	But Tom's master, Mr. Shelby, seems a decent man. He doesn't want to sell Tom. He thinks a lot of Tom. He tells Haley so.
Shelby:	Tom is a good, steady, sensible, pious fellow. He got religion at a camp meeting, four years ago; and I believe he really *did* get it. I've trusted him, since then, with everything I have—money, house, horses—and let him come and go round the country; and I always found him true and square in everything.
Storyteller 3:	But Shelby's in debt to Haley. He has to sell Tom, but the slave trader is not satisfied with just Tom. He wants even more slaves.
Haley:	Well, haven't you a boy or gal that you could throw in with Tom?
Storyteller 2:	He's seen Eliza, the young quadroon woman Shelby owns.
Storyteller 5:	She's a—quadroon?
Storyteller 2:	Three-fourths white—quadroon. Now, Haley wants her, too.
Storyteller 3:	Shelby needs the money, but he refuses to sell Eliza?
Storyteller 2:	Right. So then Haley demands Eliza's little son.
Haley:	Well, you'll let me have the boy, though.
Shelby:	I would rather not sell him. . . . The fact is, sir, I'm a humane man, and I hate to take the boy from his mother, sir.

Haley: O, you do?—La! yes—something of that ar nature. I understand perfectly. It is mighty onpleasant dealing with women sometimes, I al'lays hates these yer screachin', screamin' times.

Storyteller 3: So how does Haley handle such a cruel situation—taking a child from his mother?

Storyteller 2: He'll do anything—say anything to get what he wants. So he tells Mr. Shelby to trick Eliza:

Haley: Now, what if you get the girl off for a day, or a week, or so; then the thing's done quietly—all over before she comes home. Your wife might get her some ear-rings, or a new gown, or some such truck, to make up with her.

Shelby: I'm afraid not.

Haley: Lord bless ye, yes! These critters ain't like white folks, you know; they gets over things. . . . It's always best to do the humane thing, sir; that's been *my* experience.

Storyteller 3: Whew. That's his version of being humane? That knocked the mind right out of me.

Charles: Not a pleasant scene that, I grant you.

Harriet: But Charles, slave traders were not pleasant men.

Storyteller 5: Living in the North, like you did, Mrs. Stowe, how could you, or anyone, make up this scene?

Harriet: Oh, I didn't make it up—entirely. We moved to Cincinnati on the western frontier in 1832. There, I saw slavery for the first time.

Storyteller 3: Ohio was part of the western frontier? Ohio?

Charles: Think about it. We're talking the 1830s now—Chicago is barely a prairie dream. Covered wagons are on the Oregon Trail and heading to California. Ohio is still a new state.

Storyteller 3: But a Free State, right? Blacks were free in Ohio?

Storyteller 5: True, but right across the river is Kentucky.

Storyteller 2: Blacks definitely were not free in Kentucky. That was a slave state.

Storyteller 1: But, you know, even there some owners freed their slaves. And some slaves bought their own freedom.

Harriet: The Ohio River did separate us from Kentucky. Still, the evils of slavery clouded the very atmosphere in Cincinnati.

Storyteller 1: What did you do in this strange land—when you saw slavery?

Harriet: I listened. I read books. I read the posters advertising people for sale—human beings for sale! And I worried. I wrote a geography book, and I went on teaching in the school my oldest sister, Catherine, founded. She had wonderful plans and was a very insistent woman. Listen to a bit of one letter she wrote to me:

Catherine: Well, I am determined to establish a school in Cincinnati to raise up teachers for the West. You see, Hattie, the folks are very anxious to have a school on our plan set on foot here. We can have fine rooms in the city college building, which is now unoccupied, and everybody is ready to lend a helping hand.

Harriet:	You see? Catherine was brilliant and very determined. *(Pause)* We did, though, disagree about God—and about slavery.
Charles:	In particular, getting rid of slavery—abolishing it.
Harriet:	Talk of such abolition was all around us. Father was president of Lane Theological Seminary in Cincinnati. Unhappily for him, that school became a hot bed of radical abolitionists.
Charles:	So—practically all the members of our family were abolitionists, but they still debated the best way to abolish slavery?
Harriet:	Yes. We were terribly concerned. What was the best method to follow? Should the country emancipate the slaves all at once?
Dr. Beecher:	Or should we free them gradually?
Catherine:	Maybe we should return them and their families to Africa?
Harriet:	We had questions with no pat answers. I, too, was undecided. Then, one day, I accepted an invitation to cross the Ohio River and visit Kentucky.
Storyteller 3:	Don't tell me you visited a plantation—with slaves?
Harriet:	I did, but I saw none of the horrors I expected. *(Pause)* I heard of them, though. I heard of them.
Charles:	Tell them, Mother. Tell them about the girl who escaped.
Harriet:	It's the plantation owner's story—about a young slave, a young woman, who fled with her child across the partially frozen river.
Storyteller 3:	Partially frozen? You mean partially thawed! That's dangerous! Why would she risk her life—and her child's life—like that?
Harriet:	Desperation. Her child was about to be sold—torn away from her. Years later, I felt that same agony. I had a child torn from me—he died of cholera, not yet two years old.
Storyteller 3:	You remembered the story of the young woman and her child.
Harriet:	Yes, because I understood that young woman so well.
Charles:	Eventually her flight became Eliza's in *Uncle Tom's Cabin*.
Storyteller 2:	I see. So after your visit to Kentucky, you went home, sat down, and wrote *Uncle Tom's Cabin*?
Harriet:	Goodness gracious, no! That came twenty years later.
Storyteller 5:	Twenty years? And in the meantime?
Harriet:	I married Mr. Stowe.
Charles:	My father, Calvin Ellis Stowe—a wonderful person.
Harriet:	*(Smiles)* And a wonderful professor and preacher!
Storyteller 2:	So you had a comfortable living.
Harriet:	*(Laughs)* Anything but comfortable. You've heard the saying "poor as church mice"? That was us.
Charles:	But you had a solution. You could earn money writing. You'd been doing it for years.

Storyteller 2:	You had been writing novels?
Harriet:	Oh, nothing so grand as that. Stories and essays for small magazines, papers—that sort of thing. Still, they brought in about three hundred dollars a year, which we needed badly.
Storyteller 1:	So you wrote for money.
Harriet:	Yes—and no. I was happy writing—even when the household overwhelmed me.
Storyteller 5:	Didn't you have help?
Harriet:	Oh, yes. I needed help, especially when I had another baby.
Storyteller 1:	A regular occurrence?
Harriet:	*(Smiles)* I had seven children—which made it difficult to find time to write. But I did—and I continued to read and learn about the slavery question. I was particularly alarmed when Congress strengthened the old Fugitive Slave Act.
Charles:	In 1850—the year I was born.
Storyteller 2:	I remember that law. It said that slave owners could cross into the free states, find their runaway slaves, and take them home.
Harriet:	Dreadful! Then, one night that law struck us personally. One of our servant girls came to me in tears. She confessed she was a runaway slave and her master was pursuing her and her little boy.
Storyteller 5:	You couldn't hide them?
Harriet:	Indeed, we could not. But there was another way out.
Storyteller 3:	The Underground Railway!
Storyteller 2:	With Harriet Tubman?
Harriet:	At the time, we didn't know about Harriet Tubman.
Storyteller 5:	But you knew about runaways and the Underground Railroad.
Charles:	Of course—the secret path to Canada. All abolitionists knew about that. They directed the slaves from one safe house to another, until they gradually made their way out of the country—to freedom.
Storyteller 1:	So you were living in Cincinnati—the first stop on the Underground Railroad.
Harriet:	I don't know how many stops there were across the river.
Storyteller 3:	Well, we're finding out—especially in Cincinnati. The Freedom Center Museum's there. It tells all about the Underground Railroad, how it started, how people helped—everything. Those were amazing times.
Harriet:	And dangerous—like that nerve-racking night when my husband and my brother, Henry Ward, took steps to help our servant girl.
Storyteller 1:	Professor Stowe and Henry Ward . . . took the woman and her child in the family carriage . . . to the lonely farmhouse of a man named Van Sant, who ran one of the stations of the underground railroad. As they drove up to the house, Van Sant came out.
Storyteller 2:	Professor Stowe sang out: "Are you the man who will shelter a poor woman and her child from slave-catchers?"

Storyteller 1:	"I rather think I am," Van Sant answered.
Storyteller 2:	"I thought so," exclaimed Professor Stowe. Then he helped the servant girl and her child out of the carriage.
Storyteller 5:	That was a stop on the Underground Railroad! They were safe. Obviously, you filed that experience away, too.
Harriet:	Yes. I couldn't forget it. When I started to write *Uncle Tom's Cabin*, I remembered that escape of our servant girl.
Storyteller 4:	Okay, but not all slaves tried to run away.
Storyteller 1:	Example: Uncle Tom. Even when he's sold, he refuses to run away. Logic tells him that if he runs, more slaves—his friends, his family—will have to be sold.
Storyteller 5:	But the circumstances are different for Eliza. She belongs to the same master as Tom, but she has a child to protect.
Storyteller 4:	She can't run—yet she can't stay. Matters grow worse, especially when her husband, George, tells her what his master plans for him:
George:	He says he won't let me come here any more, and that I shall take a wife and settle down on his place. At first he only scolded and grumbled these things: but yesterday he told me that I should take Mina for a wife, and settle down in a cabin with her, or he would sell me down river.
Eliza:	Why, but you were married to *me*, by the minister, as much as if you'd been a white man.
George:	Don't you know a slave can't be married? There is no law in this country for that; I can't hold you for my wife, if he chooses to part us.
Storyteller 5:	Eliza can't say a word to George. She has to be close to tears.
George:	Eliza, my girl . . . bear up, now, and good bye; for I'm going.
Eliza:	Going, George!—going where?
George:	To Canada . . . and when I'm there, I'll buy you—that's all the hope that's left us. You have a kind master that won't refuse to sell you. I'll buy you and the boy—God helping me, I will! . . . I won't be taken, Eliza—I'll *die* first! I'll be free, or I'll die!
Storyteller 5:	Eliza can't tell him her fears for their son, but now she makes up her mind to run away. She confides in Aunt Chloe and Uncle Tom.
Eliza:	I saw my husband only this afternoon. . . . Do try, if you can, to get word to him. Tell him how I went, and why I went; and tell him I'm going to try and find Canada. You must give my love to him, and tell him, if I never see him again . . . tell him to be as good as he can, and try and meet me in the kingdom of heaven.
Storyteller 4:	Whew! Pretty sentimental, I'd say.
Storyteller 2:	But remember the time—way over a hundred years ago. Styles change. Words change—names of people, races—you know.
Storyteller 4:	And religion does enter into this book.
Storyteller 5:	The slaves have nothing else to count on. Hoping to meet in heaven seems to be their only chance for a better life. Eliza believes this. Uncle Tom, especially, believes this.

Storyteller 1: But they don't give up trying for the good life. Eliza won't. Carrying her little boy, she steals away in the dead of night. She suffers from hunger and the cold. The slave traders are on her trail—one of them is Haley, the man who bought her child.

Storyteller 2: The traders track her to an inn on the shores of the river—the river that separates Eliza from freedom.

Storyteller 3: But she hears them and sees them by the river.

Storyteller 1: She caught her child, and sprang down the steps to it.

Storyteller 5: The trader caught a full glimpse of her, just as she was disappearing down the bank. . . . He was after her like a hound after a deer.

Storyteller 3: In that dizzy moment, her feet to her scarce seemed to touch the ground, and a moment brought her to the water's edge.

Storyteller 5: Right on behind they came.

Storyteller 3: And, nerved with strength such as God gives only to the desperate, with one wild cry and flying leap, she vaulted sheer over the turbid current by the shore, on to the raft of ice beyond.

Storyteller 5: The huge green fragment of ice on which she alighted pitched and creaked as her weight came on it, but she staid there not a moment.

Storyteller 3: With wild cries and desperate energy she leaped to another and still another cake—stumbling—leaping—slipping—springing upwards again!

Storyteller 4: Can she make it?

Storyteller 5: Her shoes are gone—her stockings cut from her feet—while blood marked every step.

Storyteller 3: But she saw nothing, felt nothing, till dimly, as in a dream, she saw the Ohio side.

Storyteller 1: And a man helping her up the bank.

Storyteller 2: She's safe, isn't she? She and her child. They're safe?

Storyteller 1: Perhaps, my friend. Perhaps. That's only Chapter Seven.

Storyteller 2: And what about Uncle Tom?

Storyteller 4: He's been sold—down the river, the Mississippi, actually.

Storyteller 1: Haley has him on a steamboat headed for New Orleans to be sold again. High on the upper deck, in a little nook among the . . . cotton-bales, at last we may find him.

Storyteller 5: As we also find the gentleman, St. Clare, who had with him a daughter between five and six years of age.

Charles: Soon the little girl and Tom discover each other. Tom speaks first:

Tom: What's little missy's name?

Eva: Evangeline St. Clare, though papa and everybody else call me Eva. Now what's your name?

Tom: My name's Tom; the little chil'en used to call me Uncle Tom, way back thar in Kentuck.

Eva:	Then I mean to call you Uncle Tom, because you see, I like you. . . . So, Uncle Tom, where are you going?
Tom:	I don't know, Miss Eva.
Eva:	Don't know?
Tom:	No, I am going to be sold to somebody. I don't know who.
Eva:	My papa can buy you . . . and if he buys you, you will have good times. I mean to ask him to, this very day.
Storyteller 2:	She does speak to her father, and after he deals with the trader, Haley, Mr. St. Clare buys Uncle Tom, who now looks forward to a good life, after all.
Charles:	Not so fast. Not so easy. Death interferes, more than once.
Storyteller 5:	And promises are made and broken by death. Listen to little Eva:
Eva:	Papa . . . I've had things I wanted to say to you, a great while. I want to say them now, before I get weaker. . . . The time is coming that I am going to leave you. I am going, and never to come back! Promise me, dear father, that Tom shall have his freedom as soon as—*(Pause, then slowly)*—I am gone!
Storyteller 1:	Of course her papa promises to free Tom, but despite his good intentions, death interferes again, and Tom will be sold again.
Charles:	This time, Tom . . . and some half-dozen other servants, were marched down to a slave-warehouse, to await . . . the auction. A little before the sale commenced, a short, broad, muscular man . . . elbowed his way through the crowd.
Harriet:	He was evidently, though short, of gigantic strength. His round, bullet head, large, light-gray eyes, with their shaggy, sandy eyebrows, and stiff, wiry, sun-burnt hair, were rather unprepossessing items, it is to be confessed; his large, coarse mouth was distended with tobacco, the juice of which, from time to time, he ejected from him with great decision and explosive force; his hands were immensely large, hairy, sun-burnt, freckled, and very dirty, and garnished with long nails, in a very foul condition.
Charles:	He seized Tom by the jaw, and pulled open his mouth to inspect his teeth; made him strip up his sleeve, to show his muscle; turned him round, made him jump and spring, to show his paces.
Harriet:	The man, surly and dreadful, begins to grill Tom:
Legree:	Where was you raised?
Tom:	In Kintuck, mas'r.
Legree:	What have you done?
Tom:	Had care of mas'r's farm.
Legree:	Likely story!
Storyteller 2:	The auctioneer orders Tom to move forward.
Charles:	Tom steps upon the block. The bidding for him ends when he hears the final thump of the hammer. . . . He was pushed from the block—the short, bullet-headed man seizing him roughly by the shoulder, pushed him to one side.
Legree:	Stand there, *you*!

Charles:	Tom's been bought. He has a new master, Simon Legree, who owns a cotton plantation on the Red River.
Storyteller 2:	And mistreats his slaves, especially the women. But two young women, without hope, run away from Legree.
Charles:	Tom . . . knew all the plan of the fugitives' escape, and the place of their present concealment. He knew the deadly character of the man he had to deal with, and his despotic power. But he felt strong in God to meet death, rather than betray the helpless—even when Legree threatens him.
Legree:	Do you know I've made up my mind to *kill* you? . . . unless you tell me what you know about these yer gals!
Storyteller 2:	Tom stood silent.
Legree:	D'ye hear? . . . Speak!
Tom:	*I han't got nothing to tell, mas'r.*
Legree:	Do you dare to tell me, ye old black Christian, ye don't *know*?
Charles:	Tom was silent.
Legree:	*(Angrily)* Speak! . . . Do you know anything?
Tom:	I know, mas'r; but I can't tell anything. *I can die!* . . . O, mas'r, don't bring this great sin on your soul! . . . Do the worst you can, my troubles'll be over soon; but if ye don't repent, yours won't *never* end!
Charles:	Legree stood aghast . . . one hesitating pause . . . and the spirit of evil came back. . . . Foaming with rage, he smote his victim to the ground.
Storyteller 3:	That's a horrible scene!
Harriet:	Scenes of blood and cruelty are shocking to our ear and heart. What man has nerve to do, man has not nerve to hear. . . . And yet, o, my country! these things are done under the shadow of thy laws!
Storyteller 5:	Strong words from our author, who described herself as—
Harriet:	A little bit of a woman—somewhat more than forty, just as thin and dry as a pinch of snuff.
Storyteller 3:	But Harriet Beecher Stowe had a cause. She had a mission!
Harriet:	I did—especially after my sister-in-law, Isabella, wrote this to me:
Storyteller 5:	*(As Isabella)* Now, Hattie, if I could use a pen as you can, I would write something that would make this whole nation feel what an accursed thing slavery is!
Storyteller 3:	And that prompted you—to make people feel.
Harriet:	Yes. I said, "God helping me, I will write something."
Storyteller 2:	First published in installments, the book came out in 1852. In America alone, one hundred thousand copies were sold the first year—to the tune of ten thousand dollars.
Storyteller 1:	Logic had not moved people. Harriet Beecher Stowe's passion did.
Charles:	When President Lincoln met my mother, we heard that he said, "So you're the little woman who wrote the book that made this great war!"

Storyteller 2: The great war, the Civil War, starts almost ten years after the appearance of *Uncle Tom's Cabin*. It ends April, 1865.

Storyteller 1: Less than a week later—also in April, 1865—President Abraham Lincoln is assassinated.

Storyteller 3: That December, 1865, the Thirteenth Amendment passed:

Storyteller 1: Neither slavery nor involuntary servitude . . . shall exist within the United States, or any place subject to their jurisdiction.

Announcer: *(Enters to center stage)* Now does Harriet Beecher Stowe put down her pen? Rest on her laurels? Not this little woman. A born storyteller, she writes on—more novels, articles, stories. Mission accomplished? And then some! But, hey, read for yourself. *(Holds up copy of* Uncle Tom's Cabin*)* Check it out!

Into the Depths of Jules Verne and Captain Nemo

Jules Verne, that indefatigable Frenchman who managed to swoop together all his interests and desires into the most amazing adventure tales, was actually a very ordinary person. Ordinary in the sense of being sensible yet full of dreams.

Having been born in 1828 near the port of Nantes and on the cusp of the Industrial Revolution gave Verne the visions of shipping and ocean voyages that underlie his later trips of fantasy. His father, a man of the law, hoped young Jules would follow in his footsteps. A dutiful son, Jules went to Paris and studied law, but the drama of the stage soon infiltrated his life.

Jules Verne began to write for the stage and became part of the literary and artistic life of Paris. After he met his future wife, Honorine, at a wedding in Amiens, Verne made a so-called sensible, financial move: He became a stockbroker.

Yet the world was moving at a dizzy pace. The telegraph, canals, railroads, and steam engines were connecting a world that bubbled in anticipation. Young Queen Victoria took the throne. America struggled in the devastating Civil War. Darwin published his monumental work. A balloon flew all the way from London to Germany.

Jules Verne was fascinated. He read all the science he could get his hands on, but he found his métier in storytelling. By the time he died in 1905, Jules Verne had written fifty novels that took us *Around the World in Eighty Days*, on a *Journey to the Center of the Earth*, gave us a *Trip to the Moon*, and sent us *Twenty Thousand Leagues under the Sea* with the inscrutable Captain Nemo and his submarine, the *Nautilus*.

Sensible to the end, Jules Verne continued to serve on the Amiens city council. Still full of imagination, Jules Verne, storyteller, continued writing to the end.

Presentation of Jules Verne Script

Tracing the imagination of Jules Verne and following the trail of the *Nautilus* through *Twenty Thousand Leagues under the Sea* leads us into a script that relies heavily on a cast of boys. However, despite the lack of female integration on an imaginary submarine in 1869, the script has three parts for girls.

The readers theatre script for this voyage calls for eight readers, including the Announcer, which can be read by either a girl or a boy. Storytellers 1 and 2 (can be read by girls) flank the reader who represents Jules Verne. The other four readers (male), Captain Nemo, Aronnax, Conseil, and Ned Land, depict characters from the novel.

Stage Props

7 reading stands, if possible

7 tall stools or chairs

Hand Props

8 scripts (plus 1 for the teacher)

8 black folders for scripts

1 copy of *Twenty Thousand Leagues under the Sea* for the Announcer to show title at the end of the show

Into the Depths of Jules Verne and Captain Nemo

Jules Verne
X

1   2
X   X

Captain Nemo   Aronnax   Conseil   Land
X   X   X   X

Announcer

———◄◆►———

Announcer:	Welcome to Storyteller Theatre! Come aboard! We're ready to plumb the depths of Jules Verne, a classic storyteller, *and* ready to follow the murky trail of Captain Nemo, master of the *Nautilus* and victim of a most cruel fate.
Storyteller 1:	*(Sarcastically)* Whoa! I'm impressed already!
Announcer:	Excellent—then we're off on a fantastic voyage with *Twenty Thousand Leagues under the Seas.*
Storyteller 1:	Hold on. That's *Sea*—not *Seas*.
Announcer:	Really? Look at the French—*sous les mers. (soo lay mare)* Under the Seas. *Les mers*—plural.
Storyteller 2:	Jules Verne, being French, obviously wrote in French.
Storyteller 1:	That is so brilliant! So cool! In French! Monsieur Verne?
Jules Verne:	*(Bows) Naturellement*, I wrote *en francais.* *(Pronunciation clues: na-too-rel-man ohn frahn-say)*
Announcer:	*(Bows)* Okay. *(Announcer starts to leave)* Call me if you need help—with French, that is. *(Exits)*
Storyteller 2:	*(Smiles as Announcer leaves)* No offense!
Storyteller 1:	Why are we talking many seas?
Storyteller 2:	Well, if you travel twenty thousand leagues, you're apt to sail through more than one ocean. You do know how far twenty thousand leagues would be?
Storyteller 1:	Oh, sure. *(Thinking hard while speaking)* Twenty thousand leagues times three miles—would be sixty thousand miles.
Storyteller 2:	Correct. Enough to sail clear around the world twice—with a side jaunt to the South Pole.
Storyteller 1:	Hey, is this a story about geography?
Storyteller 2:	Actually, no. We're talking high-tech time. Grab your pencil, your pen, your calculator, and listen up!

Storyteller 1:	High tech? Hold on. I just *happen* to know when that book came out: *Twenty Thousand Leagues under the Sea*—1869. Are we talking about high tech in 1869—when the first real bicycles were built? Please—I don't think so!
Storyteller 2:	You'll see—and when you do, you'll be surprised, amazed, and overwhelmed. Listen to our author, Jules Verne. *(Indicates)*
Storyteller 1:	Okay, surprise me. I'm listening, but I'm a low-tech person myself.
Jules Verne:	Excuse me. A hundred years before bicycles, men were already flying.
Ned Land:	Leaving the earth? No good will ever come of that!
Jules Verne:	I'm speaking of exploring, sir. You can appreciate that, Mr. Land. Think of it! Men going to the center of the earth. Men going to the moon, perhaps flying in balloons—around the world in no time at all—around the world in eighty days. Think of it!
Ned Land:	I am a Canadian, sir. I plant my feet on good ole' terra firma!
Jules Verne:	But think of it, sir. Men leaving the earth. They're flying up, into the air, looking up and looking down onto Earth. Exploring!
Captain Nemo:	Ha! As Captain Nemo, I *know* there's more than one way to leave the earth. I, too, sought a different atmosphere—a different life. I found it under the waters of the world. The sea is all! . . . It is no more than a vehicle for a supernatural and prodigious existence. . . . There one finds supreme tranquility . . . independence! There I recognize no masters! There I am free! Understanding this, my friends, you may understand why I went sub-marine.
Storyteller 1:	I get it. I get it—Captain Nemo under the sea!
Storyteller 2:	Of course. But think who created him—Jules Verne. *(Turns to Verne)* Did you love the sea, sir?
Jules Verne:	I did—still do. I grew up near the sea. The smell of the great ocean winds, the constant movement of the tides fascinated me as a boy, as they do now. I saw the ships. I knew about the great battles on the water. I wondered what it would be like to travel on it—*in* it. Travel in a submarine. *(Laughs)* I, of course, am no scientist—but I could invent Captain Nemo, and he could invent the technology for a submarine—a ship that would travel under the waters.
Storyteller 1:	Give me a break! Technology for a submarine in 1869?
Jules Verne:	Not so impossible. I'd read about such a vessel: first, about the inventor in my France who designed the first submarine for your Navy. It was called the *Alligator*. Was appropriate name, I think. She was green, like an alligator, with oars like little feet to move her along.
Storyteller 1:	Some story! Where is she now?
Jules Verne:	Submerged—a wreck. She sank in 1863, one year after her launch. But even before the *Alligator*, Napoleon the Third wanted a submarine. He commissioned Robert Fulton to design one for him.
Storyteller 1:	Come on—Robert Fulton designed steamboats.
Jules Verne:	But in 1800, he was living in France, and he built Napoleon's submarine—called it the *Nautilus*. Correct, Monsieur Aronnax?

Aronnax:	Yes, sir.
Conseil:	*Nautilus*: Latin for a sea creature that moves in an unusual way.
Storyteller 1:	Oh, I see—high-tech fishes!
Storyteller 2:	Be quiet and pay attention! Let this man Aronnax speak.
Conseil:	Excuse me, Master Aronnax, I believe I can explain the movements of the sea creature—if you do not mind, sir?
Aronnax:	You may go on, Conseil. You've learned your lessons well.
Conseil:	Thank you, master. The nautilus is a small pearly-shelled cephalopod . . . that regulates its ascent and descent by the amount of gas it emits or retains in its shell.
Storyteller 1:	Oh, sure! This high-tech sea creature, this submarine of yours, Captain Nemo, goes up and down with a gas engine?
Captain Nemo:	Indeed not. The *Nautilus* I command goes up and down by means of electrical energy—electricity.
Storyteller 1:	Hold on! Electricity in 1869? Very low-tech time, I believe—no electric lights, let alone electric *motors* in 1869.
Jules Verne:	But we were dreaming of all those wonders at that time.
Storyteller 1:	Well, did you dream up atomic energy?
Jules Verne:	This is—what? *(Obviously confused)* A-tomic?
Storyteller 2:	Atomic energy. Our submarines are powered by atomic energy.
Jules Verne:	That is *très intéressant*! *(tray ain-tay-ruh-sahn)*
Storyteller 2:	What also may interest you is the *name* of our first atomic submarine.
Storyteller 1:	I know that! It was the *Nautilus*! What a coincidence. I've got the date for her launching, too—1954. That's 150 years after Robert Fulton's little experiment—the first *Nautilus*.
Jules Verne:	*(Smiles)* In my time we could only imagine the magic of electricity.
Storyteller 2:	But you weren't a scientist, were you?
Jules Verne:	Only in my dreams and in my reading. I couldn't get enough of the new experiments—the new science, the work of naturalists like Charles Darwin.
Storyteller 1:	Oh, yeah. Biology, ecology, survival of the fittest, and all that.
Jules Verne:	I did have a passion for those sciences, but my father intended me to become a lawyer, like him. So, I went to Paris, studied law, but underneath it all, I really wanted to write stories—plays for the stage. Operettas, you know.
Storyteller 1:	Frilly little operas?
Jules Verne:	I suppose you could say that. But my great friend, Alexandre Dumas (*Doo*-ma) encouraged me a great deal to write for the stage.
Storyteller 2:	Dumas. He wrote novels.
Jules Verne:	But first, plays, then novels—books like *Les trois mousquetaires*. *(lay traw moose-ka-tear)*
Storyteller 1:	Hold on. Is that French?

Jules Verne:	*Oui*, it is French.
Storyteller 1:	Can you spell it?
Jules Verne:	*Certainement (ser-tain-mahn) (Spells slowly)* M-<u>o</u>-<u>u</u>-<u>s</u>—
Storyteller 1:	<u>E</u>. I get it! *(Sings)* M-o-u-s-e—Mouseketeers, of course!
Jules Verne:	In English—*The Three Musketeers*. The adventures in that book inspired me as I wrote my plays. Oh, I studied law. I read science, but as I wrote, I began to think of adventures in other times, in other worlds.
Storyteller 2:	So you created your own three musketeers and invented their adventures in *Twenty Thousand Leagues under the Sea*.
Jules Verne:	I did. Let me formally introduce them to you—
Aronnax:	*(Slight bow to audience)* The honorable Pierre Aronnax, professor at the Museum of Paris and author of *The Mysteries of the Great Sub-marine Depths*. If you please, my servant:
Conseil:	*(Slight bow to audience)* I am called Conseil. I am Flemish—Belgian, like you say, from northern France.
Aronnax:	For the past ten years, Conseil has followed me wherever science has led me. Never a reflection from him on the length or tiresomeness of a trip. No objection to packing a bag for whatever country, China or the Congo, no matter how far off it might be.
Conseil:	Master must be reminded I live to serve.
Aronnax:	This fellow was thirty years old, and his age was to this master's as fifteen is to twenty. . . . If you'll excuse me for saying in this manner that I was forty years old?
Storyteller 1:	I'm becoming amazed—a young boy of thirty. How did you pick up that other fellow, the Canadian?
Ned Land:	*(Bows)* Ned Land—from Quebec City.
Storyteller 2:	So, Monsieur Aronnax, you, your servant, and Ned Land here embark upon an adventure. Describe what that was, please.
Aronnax:	Gladly. We were on a government expedition to track down a huge ocean monster. Sailors from around the world had seen it—been struck by it. Feared it. Our mission was to find the monster and kill it. As I told Conseil, "We are going to rid the seas of it."
Storyteller 2:	And because you thought you were chasing a sea monster—
Conseil:	A narwhal, to be exact—an arctic cetacean about twenty feet long with a long, twisted ivory tusk.
Aronnax:	Capable of ramming ships, even sinking them—which it often did.
Storyteller 2:	Hunting this huge whale, you needed someone on board who could kill such a creature.
Storyteller 1:	With a harpoon!
Aronnax:	Our frigate, the *Abraham Lincoln*, had every means of destruction. But it had even better. It had Ned Land, the king of harpooners.

Ned Land:	*(Slight bow)* Thank you, monsieur.
Storyteller 1:	Another young kid—about forty?
Aronnax:	About. He was tall—more than six feet—and well built, serious, and uncommunicative, sometimes violent, and really angry when he was contradicted. In fact, Ned showed his strong opinions when I asked him, "How can you not be convinced of the existence of this cetacean that we are chasing? Do you have some particular reason for being so doubtful?"
Ned Land:	Maybe I do, Monsieur Aronnax.
Aronnax:	Yet you, Ned, who's a whaler by profession and who's familiar with all the great marine mammals—you whose imagination ought to accept the hypothesis of these enormous cetaceans—you ought to be the last to doubt under these circumstances.
Ned Land:	That's where you're wrong, Professor. . . . I have given chase to many cetaceans; I've harpooned a great many of them and killed many of those, but no matter how powerful or well-armed they may have been, neither their tails nor their defenses would have been able to cut into the metal plates of a steamer.
Storyteller 2:	So—the sailor was right. You were trying to find a submarine. You were not chasing a monster.
Aronnax:	That is correct. *(Slight pause)* However, we did not know that at first. But when we discovered the submarine, we also discovered a monster—inside that submarine.
Storyteller 1:	Are you speaking of finding Captain Nemo?
Aronnax:	I'm afraid that I am.
Storyteller 1:	How did you find him—and his submarine? Where were you?
Aronnax:	Our frigate was in the northern regions of the Pacific Ocean. Night was coming on. Eight bells had just been struck. Big clouds covered the face of the moon which was then in its first quarter. The sea peacefully undulated under the frigate's bow. . . . In the midst of the overall silence, a voice had just been heard. It was Ned Land's and he was shouting.
Ned Land:	Ahoy there! Just what we're looking for, to windward, across from us!
Aronnax:	The sea seemed to be illuminated from below.
Jules Verne:	Fish like the pholades and salpae can, of course, produce such a light. But the men on board that frigate see something electrical that moves back and forth, then toward them.
Aronnax:	We waited. The monster moved. We followed. It raced away. We followed still, watching the light. The captain of our frigate asked Ned if he should put the boats out to sea.
Ned Land:	No sir. . . . Put on steam if you can, sir. As for me, with your permission, you understand, I'm going to take up a position under the bow rigging, and if we get within a harpoon's length, I'll harpoon it.
Conseil:	The captain obliged. The engines ran full speed ahead. Perhaps three hundred miles later, we came upon the narwhal, floating.

Aronnax:	At that moment, leaning on the handrail of the forecastle, I saw below me Ned Land hanging on to the martingale with one hand and brandishing his terrible harpoon in the other. Barely twenty feet separated him from the motionless animal. Suddenly, with a violent motion, his arm released and launched the harpoon. I heard the audible impact of the weapon *(Slowly)*, which seemed to have hit a hard object.
Conseil:	The electric light suddenly went out, and two enormous masses of water engulfed the bridge of the frigate, running like a torrent from fore to aft, bowling over men, and breaking the rigging of the masts and spars.
Aronnax:	A horrible shockwave was produced and, launched over the handrail without the time to hang on, I was thrown into the sea. . . . "Help! Help!" I shouted. . . . "Help!" This was the last cry I gave. My mouth filled with water. I struggled, drawn down into the abyss. . . . Suddenly, I heard, yes, I heard these words in my ear:
Conseil:	If master will be so good as to rest upon my shoulder, master will swim much more comfortably.
Aronnax:	With one hand I grabbed the arm of my faithful Conseil. "You!" I said. "It's you!"
Conseil:	None other, master, and at your command.
Aronnax:	The shock threw you overboard at the same time as I?
Conseil:	Not at all. But being in the service of my master, I followed him.
Storyteller 1:	What? He jumped in after you? I think I'm overwhelmed!
Storyteller 2:	I thought you might be.
Aronnax:	At this moment, in the last light of the moon which was descending towards the horizon, I made out a face that was *not* Conseil's and which I immediately recognized. "Ned!" I cried.
Ned Land:	In person, sir, and in pursuit of his prize!
Aronnax:	You were thrown overboard by the impact of the frigate?
Ned Land:	Yes, Professor, but in a luckier manner than you; I was able to set foot almost immediately on a little floating island.
Aronnax:	A little island?
Ned Land:	Yes, more properly said, on our gigantic narwhal.
Aronnax:	Explain yourself, Ned.
Ned Land:	I soon understood why my harpoon was unable to pierce it and blunted itself on its skin.
Aronnax:	Why, Ned? Why?
Ned Land:	Because that beast, Professor, is made of steel plates!
Aronnax:	The three of us climbed aboard. Then I realized we were spread out on the back of some sort of submarine boat, which appeared, for all I could tell, to have the form of an immense steel fish.
Ned Land:	So long as it sails horizontally, . . . it's fine with me. But if it takes a notion to dive, I wouldn't give two dollars for my skin.

Aronnax:	On we floated through the night. Then the day dawned. . . . I was about to make a careful examination of the hull . . . when I felt it *sink* little by little.
Ned Land:	Damn it all. . . . Open up, you inhospitable sailors!
Aronnax:	Luckily, the sinking movement stopped. Suddenly the sound of metal fittings being violently pushed came from the boat's interior. . . . A man appeared, yelped a strange cry and immediately disappeared. Soon after, eight solidly built men appeared silently with masked faces and led us *into* their formidable machine.
Storyteller 1:	Swallowed up—like Jonah—swallowed whole by the whale!
Storyteller 2:	You were rescued by men from the *Nautilus*?
Aronnax:	Rescued is one way to put it. Certainly we were pulled from the immediate threat of drowning, but we hadn't met the captain yet.
Storyteller 2:	When you did, what did you find?
Aronnax:	A man who, on our first meeting, did not speak to us. On our second meeting, that captain made our position very clear:
Captain Nemo:	I hesitated a long time. . . . Nothing forced me to offer you hospitality. If I had to separate myself from you, I had absolutely no interest in seeing you again. I put you back again on the platform of this ship which has served as your refuge. I sink beneath the waves, and I forget that you ever existed. Wasn't this my right?
Aronnax:	The right of a savage, perhaps . . . but not of a civilized man.
Captain Nemo:	Professor . . . I am not what you call a civilized man! I have broken with all society for reasons that I alone have the right to understand. Therefore I don't recognize any of its rules, and I demand that you never invoke them before me!
Aronnax:	This was said clearly and definitely. A flash of anger and disdain had lit up the eyes of this unknown, and I caught a glimpse of an awful past in the life of this man.
Captain Nemo:	I did, then, hesitate . . . but I thought that my own interests could be compatible with this natural sense of pity that all human beings have a right to. I told them, "You will remain aboard, since fate has flung you here. Here you will be free, and in exchange for this freedom . . . I will only impose upon you a single condition. Your word to submit to it will be enough for me. . . . I expect from you, even more than from the others an absolute and blind obedience."
Storyteller 1:	What was he talking about? Were you free or not?
Aronnax:	Essential question. I asked him what he meant by this liberty.
Captain Nemo:	The liberty to come and go, to see, even to observe everything that goes on here—except in certain serious circumstances—the freedom, that is, that we ourselves, my companions and I, enjoy.
Aronnax:	I began to understand—we were his prisoners. Captain, we must give up forever seeing our country, our friends, our relations?
Captain Nemo:	Yes, sir.
Ned Land:	Amazing! I'll never give my word to not try to escape.

Captain Nemo:	I don't ask you for your word, Master Land.
Aronnax:	Sir . . . you're taking advantage of us. This is cruel.
Captain Nemo:	No, sir, it is clemency! You are my prisoners following combat. . . . You attacked *me*! You came to learn the secret that no man in the world must penetrate . . . the secret of my whole existence! And you believe that I am going to send you back to this world that must no longer know anything of me? Never!
Aronnax:	So, sir . . . you simply give us the choice between life or death?
Captain Nemo:	Quite simply.
Aronnax:	There is nothing to say to a question posed in such a manner. But no word of honor ties us to the master of this ship.
Captain Nemo:	None whatsoever, sir. . . . But you will not regret the time spent aboard. You are going to travel in Wonderland.
Aronnax:	Certainly, the commander was correct about that. We explored and marveled at underwater beauties—and adventures so life-threatening, so horrible, that none of us could have imagined.
Storyteller 1:	The shark! Tell us about the shark!
Aronnax:	*(Sighs)* One day, off the coast of India, the captain provided us with diving suits and heavy copper helmets. He wanted us to observe the natives who were harvesting oysters from the deep.
Storyteller 2:	Ah, the famous pearl divers!
Aronnax:	We were watching one diver in particular, when I saw him make a gesture of terror, rise up, and prepare to make a leap for the surface. I understood his terror. A gigantic shadow appeared above the unfortunate diver. It was a huge shark that was advancing diagonally, with fire in his eyes and open jaws. I was dumb with horror and unable to move.
Storyteller 2:	I remember this part! The voracious animal, with a strong stroke of its dorsal fin, launched itself at the Indian, who threw himself to the side and eluded the shark's bite, but not the beating of its tail, for this tail hitting him in the chest, laid him out on the bottom. . . . The shark returned . . . and prepared to cut the Indian in two.
Storyteller 1:	Then Captain Nemo sees the horror! He pulls out his dagger and buries it in the shark's side. Yuck!
Aronnax:	The shark had roared, so to speak. The blood flowed out in a torrent from its wounds. The sea was dyed red.
Storyteller 2:	The captain fell to the sea floor, knocked over by the enormous mass that weighed him down. Then, the jaws of the shark opened wide like an enormous pair of shears, and it would have been all up with the captain if, quick as a thought, his harpoon in his hand and rushing at the shark, Ned Land had not struck it with the terrible point.
Aronnax:	The waves were saturated with blood. They swayed from the movements of the shark, which beat them with an indescribable fury. Ned Land had not missed his mark. It was the death throes of the monster.

Storyteller 1:	Ned Land, the harpooner—the one man who vows to escape—he saves Captain Nemo? That *is* a surprise.
Aronnax:	True, but the tables turned for them when we met the poulpes—called the giant octopi—the squids!
Storyteller 1:	Whoa! How come you're still here to tell the tale? Do I smell an escape?
Aronnax:	You might. Time and again, Ned planned our escapes. Always something would defeat us—a hurricane or too great a distance from land. Something. Then after ten long months at sea, I awoke one morning, and I saw Ned Land leaning over me. He spoke:
Ned Land:	*(Loud whisper)* We are going to flee!
Aronnax:	I lifted myself up. *(Loud whisper)* When do we take off?
Ned Land:	Tomorrow night. Will you be ready, sir?
Aronnax:	Yes. Where are we?
Ned Land:	Within sight of land twenty miles to the east.
Aronnax:	What lands are these?
Ned Land:	I have no idea, but whatever they may be, we will take refuge there.
Aronnax:	I cannot tell how we passed the next long hours preparing the light boat, preparing our souls, waiting for ten o'clock, and avoiding Captain Nemo. At last, we were ready.
Storyteller 1:	Okay. I'm nervous. Go on. Go on!
Aronnax:	We were almost to the library. The chords of the organ resonated faintly. Captain Nemo was there. . . . I was moving slowly along the carpet . . . when a sigh from Captain Nemo nailed me to the spot. . . . He came towards me; his arms crossed, silent, and gliding more than walking, like a ghost. . . . I heard him murmur these words:
Captain Nemo:	*(Speaks slowly)* God almighty! Enough! Enough!
Aronnax:	Was this an admission of remorse that was escaping in this way from the conscience of this man? Headlong, I rushed into the library. I mounted the central stairway, and . . . reached the dinghy. I got in by the opening which had already given passage to my two companions. Let's go! Let's go!
Ned Land:	Right away!
Aronnax:	Suddenly a noise in the interior was heard. Agitated voices were answering each other. What was it? Had they discovered our flight? But one word repeated twenty times—a terrible word—revealed to me the cause of this agitation on board the *Nautilus.* It wasn't us that the crew wanted! "Maelstrom! Maelstrom!" they cried.
Storyteller 1:	Maelstrom? That's a whirlpool. Certain death!
Aronnax:	The Maelstrom! Were we then upon the dangerous Norwegian coast? Was the *Nautilus* being carried into this pit at the very moment our dinghy was about to cast off?
Jules Verne:	At the flood tide, the waters pent-up between the islands of Ferroe and Loffoden are loosed with an irresistible violence. They form a whirlpool from which *(Slowly)* no vessel has ever been able to escape.

Announcer: *(Crosses to center stage, reading from book)* "It is *there* that the *Nautilus*—involuntarily or perhaps willfully—had been committed by its captain." Which was it—by accident or on purpose? And what became of the *Nautilus*? See the movie—read the book by that fantastic storyteller, Jules Verne. *(Holds up book)* Remember, it's *Twenty Thousand Leagues under the Sea. (Smiles and thinks)* Or is it *Seas*?

Index

About the Author

Ann N. Black, a native of Iowa, graduated from Northwestern University, where she received a B.S. from the School of Communication, then worked as an actress and a writer and producer of children's radio dramas. Married to a theatre professor, she, too, switched to the academic life. Her experiences as a critic judge, and from directing, teaching, and writing, led her to a M.A. in English and Oral Interpretation from the University of North Texas, then to an assistant professorship of literature and creative writing at Northwestern State University of Louisiana. She now lives close to the Rocky Mountains and continues to write for young people. *Photo by Calabash.*